PRAISE FOR THE PEOPLES BANK

"Out of all the banks with which I've ever been acquainted, none have had a more profound impact upon their community than The Peoples Bank of Ripley." Aubrey Patterson observes, "If Bobby and The Peoples Bank only focused on Ripley, then their legacy would be complete." He continues, "But they have expanded their efforts to impact our entire region of Northeast Mississippi."

*—Aubrey Patterson, Chairman of
Mississippi's largest community based bank,
BancorpSouth, from 1991 until 2014.*

"Good leadership begins with we!" As founder of one of the largest privately owned furniture manufacturers in the United States, Hassell Franklin certainly understands leadership. He said of Bobby Martin, "If I was going to paint a picture of a community minded, Christian leader, who puts his money where his mouth is, it would be Bobby Martin. He is a big-time leader!"

*—Hassell Franklin,
Franklin Corporation, founder and CEO*

"As IBM's community banking executive during the decade of the 1990s, I loved the role America's 14,000 community banks served in their local communities. Today, as many community banks are replaced by regional and mega banks, The Peoples Bank of Ripley, MS stands out as a shining star who has never lost their focus on providing top quality service to their local community. Jody Hill has done a superb job describing the customer focused role of The Peoples Bank in northern Mississippi."

*—Bob Babcock,
retired IBM community banking executive*

"The first thing that inspires me about Bobby Martin is his faith in God." At the time of this statement, Mickey Holliman was CEO of the nation's largest residential furniture manufacturer. "Just as important as his relationship to God is how he turns his faith toward others. He applies it and uses it for good."

—Mickey Holliman,
Furniture Brands International, retired CEO

The Peoples Bank

CONTENTS

Preface   xi

Celebration   1
Personal   5
Service   9
Support   15
Interruptions   21
Container   25
Square   29
Mr. Fred   33
Evidence   37
Gentleman   41
People   45
Father   49
W.P.A.   53
Lessons   57
Torpedo   61
Extra   67
Content   71
Meander   75
Help   81
Best   87

Loans	93
Mr. Shannon	97
Uniter	101
Home	105
Family	109
First	113
Photographs	117
Teacher	125
Bear	131
Move	137
Country	143
Change	147
JHA	153
Light	159
Leader	163
Cotton	167
Golden	171
Humble	175
Community	181
Return	185
Respect	189
Relations	193
Sweet	197
Education	201
Wellness	205
Theatre	209
BMC	213
Common	217

Investments	221
Reach	225
Legacy	229
Acknowledgements	233
About the Author	235

PREFACE

This book has been over thirty years in the making. As early as my teens, I became intrigued with learning more about individuals who achieved greatness: United States Presidents, world class athletes, and successful business magnates caught my attention. I read countless biographies but never considered the similarities connecting the individuals I studied. I just believed learning more about their paths would help my own journey.

In more recent years, I began to see a connection among those who reached high levels of accomplishment. Each person I admired possessed an abundant skill for leadership. With a growing appreciation for this quality and a deeper awareness of people's hunger for it, I wanted to help others become better leaders. Knowing many people respond to stories, I felt driven to write a biography about a unique person. To begin the process, I focused on the immediate circle of people who impacted my life, searching for a person whose untold story needed to be heard. Because he excels as a leader and a philanthropist in my community, one specific individual rose to the top: Mr. Bobby Martin.

Over the past 50 years, Mr. Martin worked his way up to

President and Chairman of the Board for The Peoples Bank of Ripley, Mississippi. I felt telling his story would help me learn even more from this giant, and I knew his biography would inspire others to expand their leadership skills. Mr. Martin agreed to partner with me on this book provided it focused primarily on the bank's story, not his own. So, this book is about The Peoples Bank of Ripley and its commitment to philanthropy and service. Although in a deeper way, it tells the history of their outstanding community involvement with Bobby Martin as the central character.

While Bobby Martin serves as a mentor to me, writing this book made me aware of numerous people who similarly impacted him -- people like Walter Dowdle and his wife Theolyn. Mr. Dowdle served as an executive at the Kraft Cheese production facility in Walnut, Mississippi. Because Mr. Dowdle supervised maintenance for all of the Kraft facilities throughout the South, he and his wife Theolyn stayed at the Walnut Hotel for weeks at a time. Bobby's mother Valca Martin managed the hotel and prepared meals for the Dowdles like they were part of her family. Young Bobby affectionately called Mrs. Dowdle, Tootie. After Walter Dowdle retired from Kraft, he founded a successful industrial shelving company. Mr. Dowdle supported and influenced Bobby throughout his life. When Valca Martin died in 1973, Walter Dowdle traveled several hundred miles from his home in Alabama to pay his last respects. At this writing Mr. Dowdle is 101 years old, and he and Bobby remain friends to this day.

In this book, I share the stories of other friends and family members who profoundly impacted Bobby Martin. I dedicate this book to all of these men and women who helped Bobby

Martin grow into a servant for his community. These people who influenced Bobby also inspired me and guided me to mentor others. This is the power of leadership; when we are committed to impacting the world beyond ourselves, there is a multiplication effect. True leaders not only help others to rise to the best parts of themselves, but they also equip those they serve to be better leaders as well. I hope reading this book enriches your life as well as the lives of those you hold dear.

—Jody Hill, Spring 2020

CELEBRATION

Tippah County is nestled in the rolling hills of North Mississippi that make up the southern remnant of the Appalachian Mountain range. Situated in the northeast corner of the state, it shares a border with Tennessee. The county seat is in the city of Ripley, the home of 5,000 people.

On April 25, 2015, The Peoples Bank of Ripley had a celebration on the campus of their headquarters. The gathering of several hundred people included customers, employees, industry partners, community leaders, and public officials. The parking lot of the bank was closed for the special festivities. A white canopied party tent was placed there to provide shade from the Mississippi sun.

The main entrance to the bank has an expansive balcony that protrudes from the second floor of the massive structure. From the perch of the balcony the chairman of the bank, Mr. Bobby Martin, approached the rail to address the gathering. Earlier in the day, a permanent placard had been attached to the building just above where Martin now stood. The wording on the sign read, *90 Years — Standing the Test of Time*. This was the purpose of the day's gathering, to commemorate the bank's founding in 1925.

Mr. Martin began his remarks with the cadence of a seasoned storyteller. "It seems fitting on a day that we are celebrating the bank's ninetieth birthday that somebody that has been here for 54 of those years should be the one to recount a portion of the history," Martin says in a strong voice that masks his 82 years on earth. Less of a camouflage for his age is the shock of white hair that shines like a crown to contradict his youthful face.

Martin continues by exerting his keen sense of humor, "I've been here over half of the bank's life and that is either good or bad. I'm either too dumb to leave, can't find another job, or don't want to quit. But I guess since they can't fire me — I'm still here." Martin pauses long enough to absorb the crowd's laughter. "After 54 years, you should be out of a place, but I'm really having more fun than I ever have as a banker."

Martin receives robust applause from the crowd when he explains that the bank has made a profit for each of the ninety years that they have been in business. "The bank was started by a very prominent local attorney named Mr. Fred Smith. His initial investment of $15,000 would be worth $38 million today."

Among the many speeches that day was one by State of Mississippi Representative Jody Steverson. He presented Mr. Martin with a Concurrent House Resolution commending and congratulating The Peoples Bank of Ripley upon the occasion of its 90th anniversary.

Steverson shared that after the legislators unanimously passed the resolution, he was approached by the oldest serving member in the House. "Jody, there has never been a bank that has served their community in the same way that The Peoples

Bank has. They are indeed a gift to your constituents of Tippah County." Steverson received similar comments from multiple officials that day.

The bank's mode of operation has been the same since their beginning: giving to, and receiving from, the community that they serve. Their impact includes transformational contributions to education, health and wellness, economic development, the arts, civic clubs, and community volunteer agencies. The Peoples Bank and Bobby Martin will not release the full history of their giving records. However, those close to the bank believe that the combined giving of Martin and the Bank has exceeded ten million dollars.

One example of the bank's service to their community was a $186,500 joint contribution to Northeast Mississippi Community College by Martin and the Bank in 2002. They have continued to make contributions to the endowment that provides tuition assistance to students from the bank's home of Tippah County.

On the heels of the $186,500 commitment, Martin had this to say. "I want to further the education for the young folks in this county because, in the long run, the educational process of our students has a great bearing on our community and economic development and the quality of life of our people."

But on the day of the 90 year celebration, Martin focuses upon what the bank has received, rather than what they have given. "I want to thank all of our employees, directors, stockholders, friends, and customers for what you've done to make this company what it has been for the past ninety years. Without you we would be nothing, and we realize that."

The question arises. Has The Peoples Bank given so much to

their community because they have been so successful, or have they been so successful because they have given so much? As we gain awareness of The Peoples Bank's legacy of charitable giving, the answer will become more evident for us all. One thing is certain, The Peoples Bank operates from the belief that the stronger they make their community, then the stronger the bank will be. This philanthropic commitment is indeed an effort to be celebrated.

PERSONAL

"Can I speak to Mr. Martin?"

The reply to this question is always given with a helpful tone. Absent from the response are any questions like, *Can I tell him who is calling?* Instead the request is met with a pleasant voice. "Just a moment, please."

Whether you are a salesman, a financial investor, or an hourly worker in a furniture factory, you get to speak to the longtime Peoples Bank Chairman, Bobby Martin. He does not screen his calls.

"When you call our bank, a real person, not a recording, answers the phone." He says with a bit of disgust at the thought of how impersonal automated answering systems communicate. "We don't have voicemail, and never will as long as I'm alive. I've also told them, if they get a computer to answer after I'm gone, I will come back from the grave and haunt them." He says with a snicker before proclaiming in all seriousness. "If you call and I'm not here you are invited to leave a message. I will always call you back. May not be as efficient as a machine but it's much more *personal*."

A visit to the bank is met with the same welcoming reception.

All comers are ushered into the executive's office after a brief wait, no matter the nature of their business.

The company's name and personal approach can give the perception that the bank is owned by the community. To be viewed erroneously as a public held entity is an impression the bank board is quite comfortable with having. "The truth is, as long as people are doing business with us it *is* their bank, not ours," Martin explains.

The Southern Sentinel is the longtime newspaper which supplies the headlines for all-things Tippah County. Like many small-town papers, they provide a diverse offering of news. A typical issue might cover everything from narcotic's arrest, high school sports' scores, greased pig chases, or a fifty-year wedding anniversary.

Bobby Martin goes through each copy of the bi-weekly distribution with a meticulous eye. He sends laminated clippings from articles or pictures of anyone he finds covered in a positive manner. Along with the memento he sends along a typewritten note to each recipient. The stationary has the bank's logo emblazoned along the top of the page. The professionalism with each and every letter resembles the correspondence that one would send to a prospective client or very important board member. Often included in the note are individual experiences that the bank leader has shared with the recipient. In other words, it's not a form letter and was not written by someone else. Instead it is the personal feelings of the bank's chief officer.

Such an approach to banking may sound backwards and behind the times for modern day entrepreneurs. Some banks today possess elaborate accommodations that are built upon speed and efficiency. The most cutting edge innovators boast sleek lobbies where people have been replaced by kiosks. In these settings, the customer walks up to a computer monitor and initiates their transaction. A teller will appear on the screen and assist the customer if any help is needed. The same teller has responsibility of both the walk-in as well as drive-thru patrons. This practice cuts the labor cost in half and minimizes overhead. Some would say that our very competitive economy has made such "outside of the box" banking necessary.

We live in an era of business where computers answer phones and letter writing is outdated. Aggressive CEO's spend time studying management techniques and market strategies to move their businesses ahead in an extremely competitive economy. They would probably look upon Bobby Martin's intimate approach to running a business as a "nice touch" but who has time for personal involvement in the lives of their customers. The ever present bottom line demands results.

But along with the seemingly antiquated principles of Bobby Martin, the bank has produced results that any Chief Executive would envy. They are one of the largest community banks in the state, with assets that exceed $362 Million. These are remarkable investments for a bank headquartered in a town of 5,000 from a historically impoverished region of the country. In addition, the company records 82% of all bank deposits in Tippah County. For those of us uninformed about banking statistics, it is important to note that these are mind-boggling figures. Their banking excellence is akin to John Wooden winning 10 NCAA National Championships in 12 years as the basketball coach of UCLA. Or Google's hold on the internet search engine market. Most banks would be happy to claim 20% of their market share while The Peoples Bank captures four times that amount.

It seems that The Peoples Bank did not set out to be overly successful or produce results that skewed the average. But they have made a conscious effort to focus on **enhancing** personal service more than **reducing** cost. "We wanted to make banking a personal and pleasurable experience for those we serve. In the process, people responded in a positive manner to our approach and did more business with us." Martin explains this essential ingredient to the banks success that is also spelled out in the institution's MOTTO: *Making banking a pleasure since 1925.*

The Peoples Bank has made it a habit of investing in people throughout its 90-year history. As a result, people have poured their savings into the bank with devotion. In the process, they share a personal connection. This partnership continues to be a benefit to both the bank and the customers they serve.

SERVICE

Herbert Taylor knew, like all of his co-workers, that their company was failing. However, he was only one of a few who believed that his Chicago based company could be saved. It was the 1930's and the economy had not recovered from the Great Depression.

Taylor instituted an unorthodox plan to resurrect the company. Rather than focus on the financial numbers, he took a closer look at the company's ethical approach.

Surely some of his coworkers found such a strategy laughable. They were all going broke and Taylor wanted them to reexamine their values rather than the bottom-line. Perhaps some said, "I am not interested in being nice about going broke. I will not go down without a fight. When we get back on track we can reexamine our ethics. Right now we have to try to survive."

But that was the very desire prompting Taylor's examination of his company's behavior. He believed that business ethics built upon high principles are paramount for a company's survival. So Taylor preached that a renewed passion for serving others was central to salvaging the company.

He gained this inspiration from an outside source. Taylor was a member of a service-oriented organization made up of leaders in his community known as Rotary International. Their motto was (and still is) "Service above Self." Taylor took the motto to heart. He believed the foundation of business ethics should be built upon serving others.

Utilizing his company as a working model, Taylor devised a checklist for ethical conduct he called the *Four Way Test*.

1. Is it the truth?
2. Is it fair to all concerned?
3. Will it build goodwill and better friendships?
4. Will it be beneficial to all concerned?

Rotary International would eventually adopt Taylor's *Four Way Test* as a guide for its members to evaluate their business ethics. Similarly, Bobby Martin and The Peoples Bank have not only survived for ninety years, but have also thrived by embracing an ethical commitment to serving others. "How will our actions impact the others in our community?" was the unifying question asked by Bobby Martin and Herbert Taylor.

One does not have to look very far outside of The Peoples Bank headquarters to see its thumb print within the larger community. Situated within eyesight of the bank is The Ripley High School Event Center. It is a state of the art arena that far exceeds the norm for high school gymnasiums. The scoreboard at the top of the ceiling is a massive statistical display system. You would expect to see a game-clock like this within the confines of a college complex, rather than a high school arena. At the top of the scoreboard is a modest sign that reads, "The Peoples Bank of Ripley MS."

This is a repeated theme throughout Tippah County. You will see The Peoples Bank's trademark supporting events and organizations all over the county. It seems that no one is turned down when requesting the assistance from this institution in banking.

A respected businessman in the community once approached friends with an ambitious financial request to support a local youth camp. Several who had been asked to participate declined for one reason or another, while some of the benefactors reduced their donation to fifty percent of the aggressive amount requested. The fund seeker eventually got the nerve up to make the call and set up a face-to-face meeting with his friend Bobby Martin. In his mind, it was cardinal sin number one to ever ask for a contribution over the phone. He deemed such an impersonal approach to be ineffective. But perhaps, more repulsive, he felt it betrayed Southern hospitality and was rude.

They started the conversation with lighthearted pleasantries. The caller eventually stated he wanted to come visit Martin in person. He shared that there was a need in the community that he would like to discuss. But Martin became instantly engaged and pressed his friend for more information about the cause. The organizer hesitantly gave Martin the amount that he was requesting from each possible donor. Martin listened to the request that was accidentally given over the phone. Martin replied with the coolness he had learned from dealing with thousands of loan requests in his bank. "I think I want to do this amount instead." Rather than cut the donation amount, as some had, Martin doubled his contribution from the figure requested.

A friend of Bobby Martin described his giving with the following formula. "Some people strive to give away 10% of their wealth. Bobby's probably given away closer to half of his income."

Bobby Martin will not disclose how much it has cost him to serve his community and bristles at such wording. "It hasn't **cost** me anything, serving others has **given me** more than I could have ever imagined."

When pressed for an explanation of these views that are so contrary to many in our culture, Martin shares, "The folks at Rotary really did get it right." He says this before reciting their motto by heart. "You know it's true, *one profits most who serves the best.*"

A cynical response to Martin and the bank might be: *Do they give so much so more people will do business with the bank?* Bobby Martin does not profess to be that skilled in financial forecasting. "We have just always believed in serving our community. Getting to help somebody else is my fun time."

It is important to point out here that the shareholders of The Peoples Bank have been offered lucrative purchase offers throughout the years. In other words, if money was their motive, they could have sold out years ago and cashed in their chips. But they would not have known the joy of continually pouring life into their community. "We are not interested in selling the bank and going home to count our money. I absolutely love coming to work everyday," Martin says. In fact, he has already continued his employment twenty years past the traditional retirement age.

Herbert Taylor restored his company in 1930's Chicago by serving others. The Peoples Bank has enjoyed unequaled success by sharing the same commitment to service in modern day rural Mississippi. Time and place may change, but the commitment to others continues to produce fruit. The folks of Rotary did indeed get it right. "The one who serves best profits most." When practiced with a sincere heart, the servant is mutually blessed along with the recipient. While at times the gain is financial, there's always an emotional or spiritual reward.

The next time you take in a Tippah County sporting event, attend a family's benefit for medical expenses, or a fundraiser for a volunteer fire department, you can be sure that The Peoples Bank will be there as well. Sometimes seen, and at other times working behind the scenes. All the while serving those near and far. Because they truly do embody a commitment of "Service above Self."

SUPPORT

In the 1990's, Mike Armour was serving as the president of the Mississippi State University Lee County alumni chapter, located in Tupelo. Since Tupelo is the birthplace of Elvis Presley, the small city has been visited by people throughout the world. Besides giving the King of Rock and Roll a place to be born, it also sustains quality of life for much of North Mississippi. Tupelo was the first recipient of power by the TVA (Tennessee Valley Authority) and is also the cultural and political center for Northeast Mississippi. Although it has a population of only 30,000; Tupelo services the economic viability for more than 100,000 consumers in the surrounding area.

Mike Armour assumed the leadership role for MSU in Tupelo as a gift of service to his alma mater. He received a call one day from a fellow alumnus, in Tippah County, offering him support.

"Hey Mike, this is Bobby Martin over in Ripley," was the jovial sound that came from the other end of the phone line.

Armour knew the legacy of Mr. Bobby Martin well. Martin had long been one of the most avid supporters of MSU, and was held in high regard by the university community. Martin was selected as the MSU Alumni Association's 1999 National Alumnus of the Year, and he received an honorary doctorate from the university in 2002. Mike remembered a specific gift in 1988 when MSU was seeking to add $1 million to academic scholarships. Barbara and Bobby Martin kicked off the campaign by providing a $500,000 challenge gift. The MSU President at the time, J. Charles Lee, said, "Few people have done more to advance the quality of life in North Mississippi than Bobby Martin. His work in banking and economic development, combined with a long record of leadership and service in civic and educational affairs, has touched the lives of thousands of Mississippians."

With this knowledge of Bobby Martin's commitment to MSU, Mike Armour responded to his phone call with anticipation, "Yes sir, Mr. Martin, good to hear from you."

After a few words of warm greeting, Martin got to the point of his call. "Mike, how is your scholarship status for Lee County?"

"We have an endowed scholarship that we provide assistance with each year," Mike declared without hesitation. Mike Armour still loves to tell others about the challenge Bobby Martin provided for him and the Lee County Bulldog alums.

"We have ten of those scholarships over here at Ripley. You ought to tell your buddies in Tupelo that they don't need to let little ol' Ripley out do them."

Armour couldn't disagree with Martin's assessment, but wasn't sure how he would communicate such a blunt challenge to his colleagues. Armour says with a smile, "He not only gave me the challenge, but also the support to get our alumni group running." Armour's expression indicates he knows a secret and is considering whether to divulge the deeper truth. Finally, with the enthusiasm of a child revealing to his mother the content of a wrapped birthday gift, Armour offers the answer behind his warm expression. He reveals how Bobby ended their conversation that day by sharing the following commitment.

"I tell you what I want to do, Mike. I'm gonna send you $10,000 so that you can establish another scholarship in Lee County. I don't want a big deal made out of this, and be seen as braggadocios or a smart aleck. But you can use my name if it will help you gather more support."

Bobby Martin not only challenged Mike Armour; he also gave more than verbal encouragement. He shared with Armour the same support that he has been so eager to give to many others.

Martin has maintained his commitment to his alma mater for many years. Countless students from various places have benefited from scholarship funds delivered by Martin. In addition, he has served a lengthy tenure on the University's foundation board in recognition of his abundant giving. His gifts transcend location, race, or class. He gives wherever he sees a need.

One single mother from Tupelo has been a friend and business colleague of Martin's for over thirty years. Although she is African-American and Martin is Caucasian, the two share an affection as if they were blood kin. Martin proclaimed throughout her children's upbringing, "Those kids of yours are gonna get a scholarship from me if they go to State."

The gentle lady was a single mother of three children. Martin had been inspired by her efforts to provide them with what he would call 'a good raising' on her own. He kept up with the kids, through their momma, as they grew up. All along reminding her, from time to time, of his commitment to support their academics if they ever attended MSU. The boys complied, attending MSU and receiving their tuition support. However, the youngest was a daughter and she had plans to attend Jackson State University instead of MSU. Jackson State is one of three historically black colleges in Mississippi.

When the daughter graduated high school, Martin sent funds for her college education at MSU. The mother had to make the dreaded call and explain the change of plans to Mr. Martin. She shared her deep gratitude for his generosity, but explained that her daughter had decided not to attend MSU. Martin was gracious and assured the Mom that he understood. She was comforted in knowing that she had not offended her old friend by rejecting his offer of support. She was ready to hang up when Martin asked a parting question. "What is she gonna do if she's not going to State?"

"She's still going to college, but has decided to attend Jackson State instead."

Martin paused for a moment and said. "Well that's a fine school and I hope she will have a good experience there."

She thanked him for his kind words and assumed the conversation was over.

"Well, I don't think we need to let her brothers get ahead of her. I'm gonna send a scholarship to Jackson State for her instead of Mississippi State."

Some people talk a good game, and do little to assist others who need a little extra support. Martin however, lives most often with the view that we are all on the same team. Sure, he extends preferential treatment to his alma mater. This is the place where many supported him, and he believes in giving back where he received so much. But in addition, Martin's grace transcends traditional limits like class, gender, race, and even college loyalties. Martin doesn't focus much upon the things that promote disagreement or make us different. Instead his approach is from the position that we are all in it together.

Martin understands that true support moves beyond barriers. Support can be defined as bearing all or part of the weight of another person or object. It is not simply giving verbal encouragement, but also involves putting action behind your words. Bobby Martin has indeed lightened the load of many throughout the years by giving of his own comfort to support those around him.

INTERRUPTIONS

Brother Roy is the pastor of one of the largest churches in the state of Mississippi. There's a sign sitting on the bookshelf of his private setting that reads *MINISTER'S OFFICE*. Someone once asked Brother Roy if he kept the sign there to help him remember where he works. "No, actually that sign is a reminder of what this place is not." Roy laughs and says, "Well, you know I'm a preacher, so I think the best way to explain is to tell you a story."

Brother Roy shared that early in his ministry he prided himself on being a good administrator as well as a pastor. Unlike many of his brothers in the faith, he received his undergraduate degree in Business Management. Shortly after his arrival at the big church, he established a committee structure which allowed the various ministries of the congregation to flow like a well-oiled machine. He also operated his church office with much the same discipline. The entire church staff would gather for a weekly planning meeting each Monday morning. He utilized the mornings each day of the week to conduct the daily church business. He reserved time in the afternoons for evangelism and visiting the sick. He found it very frustrating when one of his church members stopped by the office unannounced during his morning office time. It was these types of interruptions that would mess up his day, and get him behind on his to-do list.

It was during a typical Monday morning staff meeting that he got a visit from one of his favorite church members. Elizabeth was a freshman in college and had stopped by the church on her way back to Mississippi State University. Sensing this was more than a social call, he broke out of the staff meeting, and took a few minutes to visit with Elizabeth.

"Hey there, Elizabeth, good to see you. How is school going?"

"The school work is going really well, Brother Roy," Elizabeth uttered with a hesitant tone. Her body language conveyed to Brother Roy that everything was not alright. But it took a bit more small talk before she was ready to divulge the purpose of her visit.

"Bro Roy, there has been a problem to develop with my scholarship. I don't really understand why, and can't seem to get in touch with the right person to get it resolved."

Elizabeth was a gifted intellectual, but was not skilled at conflict resolution. She was comfortable arguing her opinion on a complex academic position. However, when it came to financial matters, her understanding was as vague as if she was listening to a foreign language. In addition, she did not have the gift of gab to represent herself in a way to sway others in her interest.

Brother Roy listened and was sympathetic to Elizabeth's plight. He shared with her that he knew someone in the small town of Ripley that might could help. Elizabeth had never heard of the man, and forgot his name as soon as Brother Roy mentioned it.

Truthfully, Brother Roy didn't know Mr. Bobby Martin much better than Elizabeth did. They had met on a couple of occasions because Martin was an active member of the First Baptist Church of Ripley. It was with this knowledge that Brother Roy made a call to The Peoples Bank of Ripley later that Monday morning. He had walked around the church sanctuary trying to gather up the nerve to call. This was not Brother Roy's comfort zone. Like many pastors, he is much better suited to offer help than to ask for it.

He finally placed the call and asked the receptionist if he could speak with Mr. Martin. After one ring the phone was answered by a surprising two word response, "Bobby Martin." Yes, Brother Roy had called to speak to Martin, but he felt sure that he would get a secretary instead.

"Oh, Hi, Mr. Martin. This is Brother Roy Hipsher from Center Hill," he said quickly, unable to mask his unpreparedness.

"Brother Roy from the center of the world in Center Hill, Mississippi!" Martin said warmly. "How can I help you?" Brother Roy explained the predicament of his young parishioner's financial troubles at the university. Martin listened patiently and indicated to Brother Roy that he thought he could help.

"Elizabeth sounds like an outstanding young lady. I would like to meet her. Do you think she could come see me here at the bank?"

Elizabeth made the journey to Ripley and had the pleasure of meeting Mr. Bobby Martin. As was often the case with Martin, he contributed much more to Elizabeth's cause than she expected. In addition to resolving the problems with her current scholarship; Mr. Martin gifted her with an additional scholarship from him personally. The two built a friendship on that initial visit that continues to this day.

Elizabeth has learned much from Bobby Martin about how to treat people and give of herself for others. In addition to what Mr. Martin taught Elizabeth, Brother Roy gained a similar lesson from the faith-filled banker from Ripley.

After telling this story, Brother Roy returns to the talk of the sign on his bookshelf. "That sign that says *MINISTER'S OFFICE* used to be on the outside of my door." Roy tells the story with a soft deliberate tone, "I replaced it with a placard that reads *PASTOR'S STUDY*." Roy explained that the sign change is a symbolic reminder that he is not in business, but rather ministry. The sign has been placed on the shelf as a statement that he does not work in an office, but rather a church. It is no longer administrative efficiency with which he measures his work. Now he concentrates upon how he can make himself most available to the interruptions of others.

"Before I met Mr. Bobby Martin I used to think that interruptions were the things that kept me from doing my ministry." Roy continues with the voice of a wise sage, "He helped me to learn through his actions, not his words—that the interruptions ARE my ministry."

If you happen to call The Peoples Bank and ask for Bobby Martin he will be pleased to take your call. It is interruptions like this that allow him to continue to make a positive impact upon our world. He learned long before he became a teacher to Roy and Elizabeth that interruptions are central to a full life.

CONTAINER

The semi-truck was headed down Shelby Drive in Memphis, Tennessee. Out of nowhere, a station wagon pulled out from a road named Forest Hill-Irene directly into the path of the big rig. The trucker reacted immediately and swerved to his right. It was not enough to evade the collision and the Peterbilt slammed into the rear quarter panel of the extra long car. Tragically six-year-old David Dutton was seated in the exact location where the metal crushed like an aluminum can. The little one never knew what hit him and died in the crash.

Within days, a traffic signal was installed at the intersection, becoming a lasting reminder of David's life. His grandfather, James Luna, wanted to establish a more meaningful memorial. Along with his wife Barbara, they set an ambitious goal of fully endowing a scholarship at David's school, Harding Academy of Memphis, Tennessee. Since 1952, the academy has served students of the Mid-South as a coeducational, college-preparatory Christian school.

For James Luna, the scholarship was a way to celebrate two of his passions, his precious grandson and education. He had been an educator himself for over thirty years. Mr. Luna spent his final seventeen years before his retirement in 1984 at Hillcrest High School in Memphis. He had influenced many young people with his commitment to make a lasting impact upon their lives. One of those who found himself under Luna's tutelage was eventual Mayor of Memphis, Dick Hackett. Mr. Luna also taught in Bolivar, Tennessee where he influenced the education of William Trout who would become President of the prestigious Rhodes College in Memphis.

Luna grew up in Walnut, Mississippi where he taught school for six years before he moved to Tennessee. In 1952, Bobby Martin was a senior at Walnut High School and made a lasting impression upon his teacher, Mr. Luna. "We all knew that there was something special about Bobby, even in high school," The ninety-one-year-old Luna recounts with pristine recollection. "He was industrious and was committed to success in everything he did. Besides delivering newspapers and working hard in the classroom, he was also a really good basketball player," Luna remembers. "He always wore khaki pants to school and they were ironed with a crisp seam."

Mr. Luna extended an invitation to friends and former students to join with him in contributing to the scholarship in memory of his grandson, David. It was his fond memories of Bobby Martin that inspired him to include Martin as one of the recipients of his written request. "We didn't know how long it would take us to get the scholarship fully endowed, but my wife and I were committed; even if it took us the rest of our life." Luna's surprisingly youthful voice becomes more energetic as he reminisces, "Many people gave; it was their effort, along with an extremely generous gift by Bobby and his wife Barbara, which enabled the scholarship to be fully endowed from the outset."

These days, Mr. Luna lives in an assisted living home in Memphis, just a few miles from the location where his grandson's life ended twenty years prior. When tragic events occur in life, they have an allure to make a person scornful. But Mr. Luna remains one of the happiest people you will ever meet. When asked about his positive outlook he says, "When life gives you lemons, you've got to try and make lemonade." It's that attitude which helps him to live happily and strive to find joy in each day.

Mr. Luna speaks of Bobby Martin with deep admiration, "You know he was raised in a single parent home before we knew what it was called." Luna continues, "The fact that he did not have a father in his life could have made him bitter. But he chose to use that experience to make him better, instead of bitter."

As a person who spent his professional life educating young minds; Luna appreciates the story of a teacher who once shared a life lesson with a student. It goes like this:

> *A wise teacher once instructed a chronically unhappy student to pour a handful of salt into a glass of water and then drink it.*
>
> *"How does it taste?" the teacher asked.*
>
> *"Terrible," spat the young man.*
>
> *The elder chuckled and then asked his student to join him on a brief walk. The two walked in silence to a nearby spring fed pool of water. The wise one cast his own handful of salt into the pool.*
>
> *The old man said, "Now drink from this water."*

As the water dripped down the young man's chin, the educator asked, "How does it taste?"

"Good!" remarked the apprentice.

"Do you taste the salt?" asked the teacher.

"No," said the young man.

The master sat beside this troubled young man, took his hands, and said, "The pain of life is pure salt; no more, no less. The amount of pain in life remains the same; exactly the same. But the amount we taste the 'pain' depends on the container we put it into. So, when you are in pain, the only thing you can do is to enlarge your sense of joyful things. Stop being a glass. Become a lake."

When little David Dutton died at the age of six, his family could have become consumed with the *why* of the tragedy. Instead, they focused more intently on *what*. What could they do to transform good out of the bad? As a result, the memory of David Dutton will live on forever as he continues to impact the education of young people to this day. It was David's grandfather, James Luna, who had a profound impact upon Bobby Martin. It was from this wise educator, Bobby learned to always expand his container and be more.

SQUARE

When The Peoples Bank began operations in 1925, its home was located on the Tippah County Courthouse Square. The courthouse was originally a log structure with a large oak tree situated near the entrance. The Square, as it's known by locals, has been the setting for intrigue since the county was founded in 1836.

In 1844, Tippah County's first public execution took place on the historic grounds. The execution was justice for quadruple murders that took place at the northern reach of the county. A man named McCannon was traveling near the Mississippi-Tennessee state line and happened upon the affluent Adcock family. The family of four was moving out west and invited McCannon to join their camp. Once everyone was bedded down for the night, McCannon murdered the family, including a small child and old grandmother. He took all the family's belongings and headed back to Tennessee. However, he didn't make it far. The next day a posse captured him and brought him back to Tippah County.

As McCannon lay in jail awaiting his trial, he was visited

by an eighteen-year-old aspiring writer named William. During the visit, the young man wrote down McCannon's life story and the details of the Adcock murders. McCannon was hanged a few days later, on the Courthouse Square. McCannon was bound and placed on a horse drawn oxcart with a rope around his neck that had been fastened to the majestic oak tree. On command, the horses sprang away from the tree. As the platform was suddenly taken from under McCannon, one foot dragged along the cart, causing the body to spin like a top. Before the lifeless body became motionless, young William began distributing a written account of the murderer's story for fifty cents each.

The teenage writer's full name was William C. Falkner. He would grow up to become a railroad pioneer, politician, author, and Civil War colonel. However, he is best known for being the great grandfather of noble prize winning author, William Faulkner (originally spelled Falkner). The older Falkner's adventurous life would be loosely chronicled in the writings of his great grandson through a character named Colonel John Sartoris.

Colonel Falkner's first publication, sold on the Tippah County Square, carried a bit of prophecy for his own death and entrepreneurial spirit. His close ties to the Tippah County Square would last the remainder of his life. He built a fortune there, celebrated election to the Mississippi House, and was murdered there by a former business partner. It is fitting to say, his life in Tippah County began, grew, and ended on the Tippah County Courthouse Square.

Besides a place for retribution, the square has also been a setting for local commerce. In 1893, the Square began hosting a trade day held on the first Monday of each month. It was an opportunity for the country folks and city people to conduct their business on a regular basis. Although it eventually moved from the square, it remains in existence today as the longest running trade day in America. Known as *First Monday*, it has been visited by traders from all over the world.

In 1901, The Tippah County Courthouse began processing massive land transactions for one of the richest men in the United States, Paul J. Rainey. If his wealth was measured in today's dollars, Rainey would have been a billionaire. Rainey was an avid sportsman and went on hunting safaris in the far reaches of the world. This passion sparked in Rainey a desire to establish his own world class hunting grounds at a secluded area within the States. After attending a celebrated bird dog competition in nearby Tennessee, he purchased 30,000 acres of prime farming land and pristine wilderness in Tippah County for his hunter's paradise.

Rainey died unexpectedly on his 46th birthday, September 18, 1923, while traveling on a ship from England to South Africa. In memory of his adventurous life, his sister gifted the Bronx Zoo in New York with a major contribution. This inspired the naming, and construction, of the Paul J. Rainey Memorial Gates. The gates display ornate bronze animals sculpted into the main entrance and remain a fixture of the zoo to this day. His estate also gifted 26,000 acres of land in Louisiana that would become the Paul J. Rainey Wildlife Sanctuary. Despite his luxurious lifestyle, Rainey felt most at home on the grounds of his Tippah Lodge, so the hills of North Mississippi were his primary residence until his death. His imprint upon the entire region of Northeast Mississippi is still discussed nearly 100 years after his death.

No one familiar with the history of Tippah County questions

the greatness of men like Paul J. Rainey and William C. Falkner. The County has certainly been impacted by the Square and its various residents. Now at the turn of the twentieth century, the Square was about to get a new tenant named Mr. Fred B. Smith.

MR. FRED

It's 1914 and electrical light has not yet come to Ripley, Mississippi. It's nine o'clock at night but the darkness doesn't faze the young practitioner of the law. He has an oil lamp which produces enough light for him to work well into the evening. These are the early days of Mr. Fred Smith's law practice. One day, he would become the most prominent trial lawyer in the state of Mississippi. Eventually, he would win a favorable ruling in front of the Supreme Court of the United States. Later, he would serve in both the Mississippi House and Senate. Ultimately, his colleagues would try to cajole him into a run for governor. Instead, he stayed home in Ripley where he became the founder of The Peoples Bank in 1925.

As an attorney, Smith practiced law for over seventy years. He represented some of the largest clients in the South, including GMO Railroad and Illinois Central Gulf Railroad (both of whom held the attorney on retainer). In addition, the Institution of Higher Learning Board of Mississippi utilized Smith during the racial integration of the state's university system. During the integration process, The University of Mississippi became a hotbed of protest for those opposed to admitting people of color into the school. The Associated Press accused retired United States Army General Edwin Walker of being an organizer of student riots. General Walker filed a suit against the Associated Press for false and defamatory reporting. Walker won a decision against the Associated Press in his home state of Texas and was awarded $3 million. With other suits pending from Walker, the Associated Press stood to lose tens of millions of dollars. They appealed the Texas court's decision all the way to the Supreme Court of the United States, with Mr. Fred Smith serving in their defense. Smith argued that General Walker was a public figure. Therefore, even if the Associated Press had been false in some of their reporting, Walker would have to prove malice on the part of the Associated Press. The high court supported Smith's claim and found the Associated Press was not guilty of reckless disregard in their reporting. Thus, they overturned the lower court's decision and took away Walker's $3 million verdict.

"Uncle Fred was without question the best trial lawyer in the state of Mississippi. There is absolutely no debate about that." These are the words of Fred Smith's great nephew, Bobby Elliott, who is highly respected in the field of law. Mr. Elliott worked for Smith immediately upon graduation from law school and until Smith's death in 1984. Elliott would go on to his own prominence in the legal profession, by being elected two terms as a Circuit Judge to serve the people of North Mississippi.

Smith received his bachelor's degree after only three years of education at the prestigious Milsaps College in Jackson, Mississippi. He would go on from there to attend law school at the University of Mississippi.

The University of Mississippi is affectionately known by

some for its nickname "Ole Miss." In 1974 The Ole Miss Alumni Association created a Hall of Fame to celebrate their alums. The school describes the award in this way:

"The Ole Miss Alumni Hall of Fame Distinguished Alumni Awards recognize those alumni who have made outstanding contributions to their country, their state, and The University of Mississippi through their leadership, loyal support, service, and dedication, all of which perpetuate the great name of Ole Miss. Each year, not more than five alumni are selected by a seven-member selection committee from nominations received throughout the year."

Among the past award winners are the likes of William Faulkner, Archie Manning, and Shepard Smith. When the award began in 1974, the association wanted to get it right with their inaugural selections. Among those chosen for the very first ballot was the name Fred B. Smith. He set a precedence for greatness as a part of the school's first Hall of Fame induction class.

He laid the same promising foundation as the first President of The Peoples Bank. As a young community servant, Smith worked well into the night by the light of an oil lamp. Sure, Fred Smith's passion was his legal career, but his commitment to hard-work has been embraced by every President who has led the Bank.

EVIDENCE

In December 1917, the United States Congress approved a resolution for a nationwide prohibition for the manufacture, sale, or transportation of intoxicating liquors. Just weeks later, on January 8, 1918, Mississippi gave formal support by becoming the first state to ratify the amendment. This period of national prohibition in the United States lasted until 1933 and inspired the illegal sale of alcohol, known as bootlegging. The sale of alcohol has remained illegal to this day in parts of the state. As a result, bootlegging became the prevalent criminal enterprise in the state of Mississippi well into the 1950's. Moreover, offenders often found themselves in need of legal representation.

On one occasion, Fred Smith agreed to travel out of town to represent a bootlegger. Many of the state highways in the fifties were composed of gravel rather than concrete or asphalt pavement. It was not uncommon for winter weather such as sleet, snow, or heavy rains, to make the roads impassable. Such was the case in the middle of the bootlegger's trial. Freezing weather forced the judge, prosecuting attorney, and Mr. Fred to stay overnight at the local hotel. After dining together, the three men returned to their lodging and discovered the hotel's heat supply was less than adequate. The judge called the local Sheriff and asked that he bring over a few bottles of confiscated whiskey to warm their cold bones.

The next day the trial began with little fanfare. Shortly into the deliberations, it became evident to Mr. Fred the prosecution's case focused upon the sketchy character of the accused and little upon physical evidence. Mr. Fred seized upon this weak argument. He very eloquently presented a lecture on the history and legal precedence of the necessity for strong evidence to secure a conviction. Well into his defense, Mr. Fred paused for a breath and his gaze fell upon the judge. As their eyes met, the honorable bench master extended an uninspired index finger and slowly motioned for Mr. Smith to approach. He said with an accommodating tone, "Fred, let's not be too tough on him regarding his evidence. I think we drank up a large portion of it last night."

This little joke was especially comical to Mr. Fred's friends because they knew he was not a drinker. This story also tells a lot about Mr. Fred's personality. He was a storyteller at heart, he enjoyed a good laugh, he was a relentless jurist, but could do so while maintaining a friendship with those whom he often opposed.

"He had a way with words that I have never seen in my career in law," his nephew Bobby Elliott declared. "His verbal delivery was extremely congenial and he could persuade people with a calm and cooperative spirit."

As a judge, Bobby Elliott doesn't see much of that cordial and warm interaction among competing attorneys these days. He laments, "So much of that collegial nature is lost today." Smith had a respect and love for law, but also his fellow man.

Mr. Fred Smith was an instructor for Elliott, and many more; about life as well as the law. Smith was one of the most effective attorneys of his time, but also one of the finest gentlemen. It is good to know you don't have to be mean spirited to get ahead. Good guys can win.

Gone, for the most part, are the days when people can disagree without being disagreeable. Today, people make their point most passionately by the volume of their argument. In contrast, Fred Smith persuaded by the softness of his voice and rationale of his opinion. If a person has evidence on their side, fewer words are needed. Smith chose his words wisely and the evidence was displayed in his affection for his fellow man.

GENTLEMAN

Fred Smith's success as an attorney made him a wealthy man. However, he was very conservative with his expenditures. He never wanted to flaunt his affluence in front of others. Rather than driving an expensive car to work; Smith preferred to walk. He often made the round trip trek from his home to his office multiple times in a day. As he made the short commute, he was never in too big of a hurry to pause and tip his hat for a lady or visit with a friend on the street. The walk was part of Smith's commitment to keeping himself physically fit, long before that lifestyle became popular. The walk also personified Smith's healthy balance between work and pleasure.

Although Mr. Smith had a very strong work ethic, he also took the time to care for his spiritual and physical wellbeing. It was further exemplified with his active leadership in the First United Methodist Church and extensive tenure as a Sunday school teacher. He was a committed family man who once said, "I work as hard as any attorney in the state for eleven months out of the year." The other month he would take an extended vacation with his loving wife, Elizabeth. They would travel to

Europe and exotic tropical locations. He once met Hollywood actor John Wayne in his travels. They dined together multiple times and developed a lifelong friendship.

The one luxury that Mr. Smith did afford himself was his wardrobe of fine Italian suits. He would purchase them annually and have them custom tailored. However, no one in Ripley knew the suits carried an exorbitant price tag. The Smith's had a trusted African American house keeper named Bell. She was a part of the family and not simply an employee. She took as much pride in Mr. Fred's appearance in his suit as he did.

Bell's husband, Tom, suffered from an extensive illness for many years. The Smiths provided her a flexible work schedule that allowed her to care for her husband's health care needs. Tom's fragile body eventually gave out and he succumbed to a premature death. Bell asked Mrs. Elizabeth if she could have one of Mr. Fred's old suits for Tom's burial. Mrs. Smith was happy to accommodate and instantly agreed.

The Smith's attended Tom's funeral and Fred went to view the casket. As he looked down upon the lifeless body, Fred saw Tom wearing one of his brand-new suits. He was shocked to find out Elizabeth had mistakenly given Bell his favorite suit. Later, Fred's family said they didn't know how much Tom meant to him until the funeral. He responded with his dignified southern gentleman dialect, "You can't imagine how much it hurt me to see Tom lying there in that suit." Smith enjoyed telling this little joke on himself. Perhaps it was his way of reminding himself, *he wasn't too important, and no other man was too unimportant.*

He was big enough to rub shoulders with John Wayne and common enough to gift a suit to a family friend. He was in a hurry to fight for his clients, but relaxed enough to pause for a visit on the street and take an extended vacation with his precious Elizabeth.

It seems the passion Smith had for his daily walk was more than a hunger for exercise. Perhaps it symbolized, to him, life was less of a sprint and more of a marathon. He continued practicing law into his nineties, maintaining his integrity and love for others throughout his walk through this life.

PEOPLE

Hard work, integrity, humility, and concern for others. These are the attributes that propelled Fred Smith to become one of the most successful attorneys in the south. It was these same qualities that inspired Smith to give birth to The Peoples Bank in 1925.

As a man with substantial financial strength, Mr. Fred was often approached by friends or family members humiliated by having to ask him to borrow money. Smith must have reasoned how much more dignifying it would be if they could seek a loan in a professional manner.

These were the days when few people in rural Mississippi utilized banks to borrow money. It was the merchants who sold farm supplies that carried much of the credit. But if a man wasn't a farmer; there was no clear process for him to receive a loan. Smith saw this need and was driven to establish The Peoples Bank.

Just a few short years later, the United States stock market crash on October 29, 1929, had a devastating effect upon the banking industry. During the first ten months of 1930, 744 banks failed. Frantic consumers began withdrawing funds in mass quantities, known as *bank runs*. This practice enhanced the economic collapse; resulting in more than 9,000 total bank failures by the end of the decade.

It was during this volatile financial climate that Mr. Fred Smith paid a personal visit to most of his banking customers. He made a vow that if they kept their money deposited in The Peoples Bank, he would personally guarantee every dime that they had invested. The people of Tippah County knew that Mr. Smith was a man of his word and gained confidence in his calm demeanor. Smith would later declare to confidants that this was the most foolish business decision he ever made, but he felt it was the right thing to do on a personal level. Sure, Mr. Smith paid a high price financially to keep his investors from losing any of their money, but he gained respect and loyalty from the people of Tippah County. While banks closed all around, the Peoples Bank continued its operations and maintained a profit throughout the Depression and every year since.

In 1950, Smith sold a majority of his ownership of the bank to L.E. Watson. However, he remained a major stock holder and continued to have a positive impact upon the bank as a member of the Board of Trustees for the remainder of his life. Mr. Fred's nephew, Bobby Elliott, would eventually join the bank board in his uncle's place. Elliott continues to offer the warm and wise counsel of his uncle to this day.

Perhaps one of the greatest gifts of leadership that Smith possessed was understanding his limitations. He shared the story of a colleague in the legal practice who had risen to the position of federal judge. On one occasion, the judge called Smith into his chambers and asked a favor. "Fred, if you ever feel that I get to a stage in age in which I am no longer an effective jurist, I am asking you to inform me."

Smith never forgot this assignment and the importance of understanding one's limitations. Surely, this lesson influenced Mr. Fred's decision to sell his majority ownership in the bank in 1950. He understood that the bank needed more leadership than he could supply as a full-time attorney and part-time banker.

In 2014, the City of Ripley constructed a new baseball and recreational park. The property for the park was graciously given to the city by a grandson of Fred Smith named Fred Fortier. The Peoples Bank complimented the gift of Mr. Fortier by contributing $300,000 to support construction. Today, the complex is named the *Fred and Elizabeth Smith Memorial Park and Recreational Facility*.

Bobby Elliott lives in a quiet, upscale neighborhood that is situated just a few hundred yards from the park. Traditional placement of the noise of kids and bright lights would be an annoyance. But to Bobby Elliott his new neighbor is a welcome memorial to his Uncle Fred Smith.

In 1925, Mr. Fred started the bank because he saw a need in his community. He lost a lot during the depression so that his customers would lose nothing. In the years since, the bank has continued his legacy of serving his community. Who could have imagined that his initial cash investment of $15,000 would be worth $38 million today?

"I have never known, nor do I ever expect to know another man like him," Judge Bobby Elliott once said of his uncle. "His intellect and capacity for work is unequaled, and is matched only by his compassion and genuine concern for people."

It was this *genuine concern* for people that inspired Mr. Fred Smith to found a bank. Could he have named the bank anything else? It is indeed The Peoples Bank.

FATHER

In February 1933, The Peoples Bank was still feeling the effects of the Great Depression. But the day before Valentine's there was celebration in the family of Valca and Elijah Martin. Their first son, Bobby, was born on February 13, 1933. With three older sisters spaced five years apart, he would forever be the baby boy of the family. The family of six made their home at 205 Middle Tyndall Street in Ripley for the next five years. But In 1938, the family suffered an event that left them fractured forever.

When Bobby was just five years old, Elijah came home one morning after a night of heavy drinking and announced he was leaving for good. He had made this proclamation before while intoxicated. But this time it was different, and for one of the few times in his life, he kept a promise made to his family.

Bobby Martin was so young when his father left that he has very little memory of the events that left him fatherless. "I didn't have a daddy," he says when explaining the dynamics of his family. "He moved off up north and drove a bus for *Trailways* or somebody." Bobby Martin did not give the name of a city to which his father moved but just described it as "up north." The location of his father's adopted home matters little to Martin now; it was the one he left that had the lasting effect upon young Bobby.

After Elijah left, Valca Martin embraced the role of having to be both parents. She never let the kids make excuses or feel sorry for themselves because they didn't have a daddy. From the earliest days, she taught Bobby the importance of doing what was right.

Like their mom, each sister provided their own positive impact upon Bobby as he grew up. In addition, the Martin girls would all marry men who gave Bobby a healthy male role model.

The oldest sister was Virginia and she married J. P. Coombs. Mr. Coombs taught Agriculture at Tippah-Union High School. He had also established a distributorship of anhydrous ammonia that was used by local farmers to provide essential nutrients to their crops. He would later create Coombs Gas, a major dealer of liquid propane that remains to this day, an integral supplier of fuel for farms and rural homes in northeast Mississippi.

The next oldest was Georgia, who married Cecil Crook. They relocated to Memphis shortly after their marriage. Cecil worked his entire career as a pharmacist for Walgreens Pharmacy just across the Mississippi state line.

The youngest girl was Peggy and she shared her life with Bobby Marvin. Mr. Marvin was a compressor operator for Tennessee Gas and Transmission Company at their Portland, Tennessee facility.

When Elijah moved back south in 1984, it came as a surprise to Bobby and the rest of his family. "He didn't return home until he was ready to die." Bobby Martin makes this comment with a tone of introspection. Maybe pondering the possibility that his father was accepting death as a source of relief by describing him as, "ready to die." Perhaps even now Martin is still hopeful that there was some degree of remorse in his father for being absent from his family's life.

The senior Martin had acquired cancer and it was attacking his frail organs, which were already weakened by years of abuse from the bottle. His current wife would call Bobby and his sisters with updates on his condition from their new home in Memphis, Tennessee. He needed someone to take care of him but he couldn't bring himself to call on his kids now. So, the wife reached out to the son who her husband had left so long ago. Now after a 45-year absence from his life, Bobby Martin had a decision to make regarding his prodigal father.

Bobby Martin believes in people and their capacity to change. But he understood how the hurt was too deep for his mother to ever forget. "Divorce is so destructive. People oftentimes take the pain to their graves. Momma never did get over the pain." Valca Martin was the most influential person in Bobby's life. He didn't want to offend his mother, but he reasoned that caring for his father was what family does. So Martin somehow rose above the void his father created in his own life to fill the emptiness the elder now had. "My sisters and I took care of him till his dying day. We paid all the bills and made sure he was comfortable till the end." It wasn't so much about doing what was deserved, but what was needed. Bobby Martin has always been a man whose actions were determined more by whom he was, than who he was doing it for. It has become clear that although Bobby Martin never had a father, Elijah Martin certainly had a son.

W.P.A.

In 1935, United States President Franklin D. Roosevelt signed into law the Social Security Act. The law provided the first ever federal assistance to the elderly and people living in poverty. Prior to this event, financial support was often administered through local county governments. One such relief outlet was an institution known as the *Poorhouse*. People who had no ability to sustain themselves were given food and housing at these county-run agencies. Most of the sites were built on farms which assisted with the complex's food expenses. The accommodations were harsh, at best, and the able-bodied tenants were called upon to work in the fields.

    The Social Security Act was part of President Franklin Delano Roosevelt's *New Deal* campaign. The plan's motive was to strengthen the nation's fragile economy. Historian Carol Berkin explains the *New Deal* in this way, "The programs were in response to the Great Depression, and focused on what historians refer to as the '3 Rs', Relief, Recovery, and Reform: relief for the unemployed and poor, recovery of the economy to normal levels, and reform of the financial system to prevent a repeat depression."

A central component of Roosevelt's strategy was the establishment of the Work Projects Administration (WPA). From 1935 to 1943, The WPA spent $10.5 Billion and employed 8.5 million people. The program's goal was to provide a job for at least one unemployed person in each household. The workers built bridges, roads, parks, airports, and public buildings.

When Valca Martin unwillingly became a single mother in 1938, she moved with her four children to Walnut, Mississippi. This was her hometown, located 15 miles north of Ripley. She was able to take up temporary residence there with her parents Mr. and Mrs. L.B. Hobson. Although he grew up in a small town, Bobby Martin witnessed firsthand the impact of the WPA. He recalls, "I remember when the WPA came to Walnut. They worked on the roads, sidewalks, and public buildings." The WPA also provided operational funds for the public library where Valca Martin would find employment.

When implemented, not everyone was a fan of Roosevelt's pet project known as the WPA. Some detractors feared an abundance of government employees would lead to communism. They also argued that the inefficiency of the WPA created poor work habits. It was these types of opinions that spawned naysayers to proclaim that WPA really stood for *We Piddle Around*. The WPA may have been an easy target of criticism for those removed from the harshest effects of the Great Depression. But during this bleak time in the American South, Valca Martin knew people who were forced to eat squirrel just to survive. To her the WPA was no laughing matter. Instead, she was grateful for the food it placed on the table for her family of five.

In addition to Valca's parents living in Walnut, she also had a sister there named Lassie. Along with her husband, Everett Wilbanks, Lassie owned much of downtown Walnut. One of the Wilbanks' property holdings was a building that housed the town's library, along with a hotel and restaurant. The Wilbanks discovered Valca Martin to be a good manager and hard worker at the public library. Therefore, they asked her to oversee the hotel and restaurant housed there as well.

The Wilbanks's would ultimately become the wealthiest couple in Tippah County and the first millionaires Bobby Martin ever knew. In addition to owning much of downtown Walnut, they also controlled the town's water and sewer system. Their rise to great wealth began with a modest operation in the lumber business. They purchased raw timber from some of the numerous loggers residing in the hills of northeast Mississippi. The timber was processed into lumber which was utilized in home and building construction. In the late 1930's, Lassie and Everett bought such a huge amount of lumber that it almost broke them. But within a few years, banking on lumber paid off for the Wilbanks with the start of World War II. The war effort created a shortage of building materials throughout the nation and the Wilbanks' were primed to capitalize. "They had lumber stacked up on both sides of the road all the way from downtown Walnut up past Harmony Baptist Church," Bobby says, explaining that the plethora of repurposed trees could be seen stretched for miles. "They bought it for $25 per thousand board-feet and sold it for $150 per thousand board-feet."

In 1938, Valca Martin could've easily ended up in the Tippah County Poorhouse with her four children. But driven by a strong work ethic, all Valca needed was a chance to make it as a single mother. She was given that opportunity by a loving family and the assistance made possible by the Social Security Act. No, the WPA never did become a laughing matter to the Martin family, but it did help them to smile a little more often.

LESSONS

It's a beautiful afternoon in the fall of 1942. A Ford pickup spins gravel leaving the hotel in downtown Walnut. From Main Street the truck turns left onto U. S. Highway 72. Being one of the few paved two-lane roads in the area, it's the quickest way out of town.

The driver is a handsome, square-jawed young man, with a head full of hair perfectly manicured. Despite his youth, he has a distinguished appearance that makes him stand out in a crowd. His passengers are two young boys: one black and the other white. While there was a clear separation between the two races in the 1940's, the boys had yet to notice. The youngsters are just beginning their primary school education, but a lesson will be taught on this day that will last a lifetime.

A few miles out of town, the woods lining the road become suddenly dense. The sky above is a soft shade of blue, while the trees all around are bursting with orange, red, and yellow leaves. The trees are dancing in the wind, as if the forest yearns to be heard. The driver takes a sudden turn onto a small pig-trail that leads to Hughes Lake. He wastes no time driving down the rough field road. The instructor has brought along his favorite tool for the lesson. It's a long firm rod made of cane. It has the strength to withstand the sudden force that is soon to be placed upon it. While some may call it a rod, it's best known in these parts as a cane pole. There are fish to be jerked from the water and this is the weapon of choice.

The fishing instructor is a recent graduate from Mississippi State University who earned a degree in dairy science. His name is Luke Davis, and he is the plant manager for the Kraft cheese production factory in Walnut. He grew up one county over in the town of Myrtle. His long hours at the Walnut plant required him to occasionally stay at the Walnut Hotel. That's where he first met his fishing partners: little Bobby Martin and his friend Charles. Charles's momma worked at the hotel with Valca Martin, and the two boys were the best of friends.

Today, Bobby Martin remembers their first fishing trip well. "After we had been fishing a while, Charles and I still hadn't caught anything," he says warmly. "Luke slipped around when we weren't looking, and put two of the fish he had caught onto our hooks," Martin shares the memory with a big smile. "Me and Charles pulled those fish in like we were old pros." There's an ancient proverb that says, *give a fish and feed for a day; teach to fish and feed for a lifetime*. It's the skilled instructors, like Luke Davis, who know the secret to joy on the pond bank. A kid has to catch a fish every once in a while, or they'll eventually give up the sport. It's likely that Davis had also noticed Bobby's tough luck in life, and he wanted to help with those odds as well.

Within a few years, Luke Davis would supervise all of the Kraft Cheese plants in Mississippi, Alabama, and North Carolina. He would later become Kraft's production manager for their Central, Western, and Southern divisions. Eventually, he moved to the company headquarters near Chicago and led all Kraft manufacturing facilities as the Senior Vice President for Production. He would finish his career as President and CEO of Kraft's vegetable oil refining and sales division located in Memphis, Tennessee.

Throughout his career, Luke Davis made million dollar decisions on behalf of his company. In contrast, the value of his investment into the life of Bobby Martin is not easily calculated. Luke took a special interest in Bobby, because the youngster didn't have a father at home. By frequently spending time with Bobby, Luke shared affection in a way that words cannot express. His spirit of encouragement also helped Bobby's self-confidence grow. As he grew up, Bobby personified Luke's love for young people, and had his own nurturing influence upon many children and youth.

On that fall day in 1942, Luke gave Bobby a short lesson in fishing that lasted an afternoon. However, his numerous lessons about investing in the lives of young people have lasted Bobby a lifetime. As the night draws near on the fishing trip, the wind dies down, and the woods become motionless. The sun sinks lower in the sky, and the trees cast long shadows across the lake. Like the trees surrounding the lake, Luke Davis's impact upon this world grew even bigger than himself. Despite their best efforts to be seen, the trees on this day never made a sound. But fortunately for Bobby Martin and many more, the long shadow of Luke Davis still has a voice to this day.

TORPEDO

On December 7, 1876, a steam engine locomotive pulled into the little village of Hopkins, Mississippi. At this regular stop, the train would resupply with the raw materials needed to make the steam engine turn: water and wood.

On this day, the train had a special delivery for the Christmas season. The unique cargo contained the same qualities used to move the train. But the bare essentials, of *water* and *wood*, had been refined for a different kind of fuel. The end result was a barrel of Kentucky's finest bourbon whiskey.

As the train reached the stop, the engineer declared his cargo. "I got a little something special for Mr. Silas Hopkins."

The platform worker knew Silas well. He began performing his duties of resupplying the train with wood and water. "Hum, Silas is my kin, but he don't live here."

The engineer checked his paper, "Says here: one barrel of whiskey to be delivered for the store owners Silas and John Hopkins."

"Yep, they own a store alright,"The worker snickered. "But it's back down the track where you just came from in Hopkinsville."

"The ticket says the store's in Hopkins," the engineer pressed on.

The laborer didn't know a lot about the intricacy of railroad travel, but he knew where he was. "Mister, I cain't argue 'bout whas' on yuns paper…all I can tell ye…is 'at store ain't here."

By now, several local dignitaries had arrived to provide input on the situation. Eventually, the engineer began the unproductive task of backing-the-train-up one mile to the proper delivery point. Just as he made his way out of sight, the train-boss gave one final and lasting observation. "Hopkins and Hopkinsville one mile a part—sounds like somebody needs to change their name."

Since the railroad industry had helped identify the problem, the local fathers settled on a solution that was sure to connect with train engineers. Standing near the train-stop in Hopkins was a grove of Walnut trees. So, the northern most town in Tippah County would henceforth become known as Walnut.

Major General Alben Hopkins of the Mississippi National Guard (retired) tells this story well. It was his family who settled the area, after they purchased 20,000 acres of land from the Chickasaw Indians in 1872. Like Bobby Martin, Alben grew up in Walnut and they share a genuine affection for one another and their hometown.

Alben Hopkins was born 65 years after the town's name changed, but the railroad had remained central to the economic viability of Walnut. "My father was the Postmaster, and he would take me down to the train track at 5 o'clock in the morning," Alben recounts warmly. "Dad would hold me up and let me hand the mail pouch over to the train engineer." By this time, Walnut was no longer a regular stop for the train. Instead of stopping, the iron engine would slow to a crawl through town, so the mail exchange could take place. "I'll never forget sharing in that experience with my dad."

Bobby Martin was already eight-years-old when Alben was born, in 1941. The downtown area, had continued to build-up around the railroad. As the major transportation system of the day, Bobby explains how the track was under frequent maintenance because of its heavy usage. "Anytime they worked on the track they would put little flares on the rail known as *torpedoes*."

The *torpedoes* were small dynamite charges, wrapped in red paper, about the size of a book of matches. They were attached to the train-tracks with two lead straps, the width and length of a cigar. Scrap pieces of the lead could be found all along the railroad from years of maintenance and track repairs. Sadly, the word *torpedo* was about to take on a much darker symbol in American History.

On December 7, 1941, Japan launched a surprise attack on the United States military base at Pearl Harbor, Hawaii. Among the various aircraft sent by the Japanese were forty B5N Kate Bombers. The bombers carried unmanned water rockets known as *torpedoes*.

This warhead played a central role in sinking, or damaging, all eight of the U. S. Navy battleships moored in Pearl Harbor. Hundreds more boats and aircraft were incapacitated in the surprise attack. 2,403 American soldiers were killed and another 1,178 wounded from the horrific event.

Martin remembers the fateful day that the nation was informed of the attack. "My grandparents had an old battery operated radio. We had eaten Sunday lunch and were listening to the New York Giants and Brooklyn Dodgers football game." The game had a local appeal because Mississippians: Jim Poole, Bruiser Kinard, and his brother George were playing. "They broke-in to the game with the news report that Pearl Harbor had been bombed." For the next several days, the family remained close by the radio. Young Bobby was afraid the world was coming to an end. Within days the United States was an active participant in World War II.

During this dark time Americans came together in one accord. "Everyone put their personal interest aside for the good of the country," Martin says. "Everything focused around supporting the war effort."

One display of the wartime spirit had a direct influence upon eight-year-old Bobby Martin. In Walnut, a storage area was designated for people to deposit scrap metal. The materials would be transformed into munitions to support the war effort. Bobby remembers, "People would save their tin vegetable cans. They would cut-off the top and bottom of the cans and then mash them flat." This made for better storage of the cans.

While tin was valuable, lead became the most precious metal of all. Bobby took a personal interest in the effort. "I wanted to help win the war," Bobby says with humility. "I knew about all the lead left on the railroad tracks from used torpedo flares," he says about the safety devices. "I walked miles along the track picking up scrap lead and carrying it back to town."

There was once two separate communities in Tippah County, known as Hopkins and Hopkinsville. They eventually became known by one name: Walnut. I'm sure it took time for the people to embrace being a part of something together. Perhaps they found strength in numbers, or the fact that the common good was more important than what separated them. Ultimately the citizens of these two communities celebrated what united them, rather than focusing upon what separated them. It was that same spirit that united our country in WWII.

EXTRA

"Extra! Extra! Read all about it!" These words became synonymous with the newspaper industry in the mid-nineteenth century. Whenever exceptional events developed in the course of a day, the print agencies would distribute special editions to cover the breaking news. Young people, known as *newsboys*, would take to the streets with bundles of papers proclaiming the catchphrase that remains familiar a century and a half later.

Although the phrase remains, the actual need for extras in the newspaper industry started to die out around one hundred years ago.

By the 1920's, commercial radio had become the preferred medium for the delivery of breaking news. During the World War II years from 1942-1945, Bobby Martin remembers his family hovering around the radio for the evening update from the war front. "We thought the world was coming to an end, and I guess it could have."

By spring of 1947, the war threat had ended and Bobby Martin was fourteen years old. The family had recently acquired a Big Ben Twin Bell alarm clock that was a thing of beauty. The polished steel casing gave it a shine unlike anything else in the house. The simple white clock face deferred all attention to the black arms and numbers it prominently displayed. This was one of the first models produced after Westclox resumed manufacturing clocks in 1945. Westclox, like other suppliers, had ceased production of consumer goods during the World War II years. Instead, they dedicated the full capacity of their factories to assist in the war effort.

Although the entire family utilized the clock, it was set to sound its alarm at 4 a.m. each morning for the man of the house. Young Bobby would creep out of his Walnut, Mississippi home in these wee hours each morning making a conscious effort not to awaken anyone else in the house. Minutes after his departure, he would meet a *Film Transit* delivery truck loaded with newspapers of the Memphis based *Commercial Appeal*. Once an allotment of papers had been loaded onto his bicycle, he began delivering the morning news throughout the local neighborhoods.

This was one of four jobs that fourteen-year-old Bobby held-down to help support the larger family. On one particular day, it was cold and raining. Young Bobby was peddling as fast as he could against the wind and driving rain. He reached his first stop and dismounted the bike. He ran to the front porch, opened the screen door, and placed the newspaper in the only dry spot in the house's exterior. He would continue this exercise for every stop that day. It was not part of the job description for the carrier to place the papers upon the porch on rainy days. Most deliverers battled the rainy days as quickly as possible. Each paper was housed in its own plastic wrapping and could be thrown to a location on the lawn free of puddles. Sure, the paper would end up a little damp but a dry paper was not expected on a rainy day.

"I think back now of that fourteen-year-old boy and wonder why he did that," Bobby Martin says this with a bit of a chuckle in his cadence. This extra effort as a young kid would set a precedence for his work ethic for the rest of his life. He never has been a person who gave minimal effort, to just get-by. He possessed a commitment to excellence even as a child. His is a rational logic: If you are gonna do something, even if it is delivering papers, do it with your best.

"When I was fourteen I carried the paper route, worked at Mr. Boyd's drug store, and Doyle's Grocery. Then on the weekends I sold popcorn and cokes at the movie theatre." He says this as if a kid working four jobs was the norm.

"After the movie had started I would slip up to the balcony and sit with the black folks. I received a lot of education about the ways of the world at that theatre," he says with a snicker.

Martin has a quick wit and a robust sense of humor. He is a storyteller who can spin a yarn so fluidly it's not clear when he has doctored the details or is reciting exact events.

"Once we were showing a picture and there was a man who was sprawled out over several seats near the back of the auditorium," Martin says while spreading his arms and slouching down in his Leather desk chair for animation. "It wasn't anything for people to slip-in a few beers to drink in the dark auditorium. Somebody asked him to sit-up so they could have one of the seats. He just grunted or moaned something back at them under his breath. They got the town deputy in there to take care of him. We had a small town where everybody knew everybody and this guy was a stranger to the officer. He never moved while the cop was talking to him and remained sprawled out over three chairs with his eyes closed. Finally, the policeman asked him where he came from and the man rubbed his back in pain and said, 'the balcony.'" Martin gives a hearty laugh at his own joke.

His personal space at the bank is not an elaborate showplace fitting of a chairman for one of the most successful financial institutions in the state of Mississippi. His work area is designed around functionality rather than luxury. There are various bank projects compiled in bulky packets on top of his desk, this is a working office. He has not had a sick day in more than 50 years of employment at The Peoples Bank. Well into his 80's, Bobby still works six days a week, giving the extra effort of a man two decades his junior. "I love coming to work every day," he says, unable to contain his affection for the institution and the people it serves.

Martin began our conversation on this day with a question. "Why did I always put the paper behind the door on rainy days?" It seems his passion for hard work now and his willingness to serve when he was a kid have a central motivator. He always has loved people and serving them. He must see work not as a way to get, but as a way to give.

The twin bell alarm clock has been replaced by a modern day digital version. Although the model has changed, it still serves the same purpose—allowing him to rise early so he can give a little extra to each day. Bobby Martin began his working career seventy years ago and continues to this day. Throughout these years of service, he has poured an abundant amount of joy into others. His extra efforts will indeed have a timeless effect upon our world.

CONTENT

The National Interstate and Defense Highway Act was signed into United States law by President Dwight D. Eisenhower on June 29, 1956. Following World War II, Eisenhower felt that limited-access four lane roads were essential for national defense. The President argued, if the American homeland was attacked by foreign invaders, the military would need the capability of transporting forces across the country in an efficient manner.

The mass construction project also enhanced automobile transportation throughout the nation. Until that time, family vehicles were a rare commodity, and were used mostly for local commutes. Thus, in the 1940's, more lengthy travel needs were largely conducted by the commercial bus industry. Trailways Transportation System had developed regional intercity travel options to compete with national powerhouse, Greyhound Lines. One such Trailways route ran between Jackson, Tennessee and New Albany, Mississippi. As a result, Walnut, Mississippi like many small towns, was equipped with their very own bus station.

In the fall of 1948, Bobby Martin began his education as a

ninth grader at Walnut High School. The local bus station had become an after-school hang out, since it was within walking distance of the campus. The young patrons could acquire milkshakes and burgers at the Bus Station Cafe. There was also a pool table to service entertainment needs. Bobby Martin's mother had issued a strict forbiddance of pool playing by her son. He respectfully complied but gained a thorough understanding of how the games were conducted. "As long as you were winning, you kept playing. Each new challenger had to buy the balls for the next game. So, if you were handy with a cue stick, you could play pool all day with a few coins." Occasionally, games were played for money and some were well equipped as sandbaggers. The standard mode of operation by these particular pool sharks was built upon deception. They would play games, just barely winning each time, as the stakes raised until they had taken all of the challenger's money.

Bobby Martin began a quick friendship with a young lady in his class named Barbara Moore. She was soft spoken and never said much at school, but Bobby found her to be a little more talkative in the one-on-one visits at the bus station. Before long the couple entered into the first official romance for either of the young teens. This was the beginning of a relationship that would lead to a sixty-year marriage celebration in December of 2015.

"I could not have asked for a more supportive wife," Martin says now, looking back upon his life. "If I called her right now and said we need to go to the funeral home to visit a bereaving family, she would say, 'Okay, I'll be ready in fifteen minutes.'"

Barbara downplays her support role with genuine humility. "My momma always went along with my daddy's ideas, and I guess I felt that is how a wife should act. They sure don't act that way anymore." She says, beginning a laugh, "I don't guess I would either if I was to come up now." She says this alluding to the vast cultural differences in the sixty years that have passed since her wedding day. "I guess I started-out on the wrong foot from the get-go," she says with a gentle chuckle.

This is not to say that they don't disagree at times, and Mrs. Barbara doesn't speak her mind. "Sure we disagree. You can't be in any kind of relationship without seeing things differently. He asks my opinion oftentimes, and I never hesitate to tell him what I think." Her wisdom flows out with every new statement she makes, "But I don't usually make any waves, or big demands, when we disagree." She pauses to reflect further and finishes, "At the end of the day he's gonna do what he wants, and I'm gonna support him."

Barbara has always enjoyed reading, and was a good student throughout her school days. She once worked hard on a book report and was disappointed when she received a "B" as her grade. Bobby had a different teacher and his love struck girlfriend allowed him the usage of her paper for an outline for his own assignment. Her intentions got lost in translation to Bobby, and he turned in the exact same paper. When he got the paper back he was rewarded for his hard work with an "A." Perhaps the teacher instructing Bobby's class had a relaxed grading scale, but there may have been a more personal reason. It seems that this experience speaks to Bobby's persuasive nature and enduring personality, already evident at a young age.

Years later, when Bobby and Barbara married, they would attend banking functions and Bobby would "work the crowd," in the words of his wife. She was content to simply be present, and show her support in the background. "Early into our marriage,

I didn't like all the social functions. I am a naturally shy person and am not real comfortable in large crowds." But over time she grew more comfortable with public life.

Barbara's contentment has been essential to the success of their life and philanthropic spirit. It seems Bobby's business and people skills could not have found a more harmonious fit. A less content person would not have embraced a lifestyle so contrary to her comfort zone. But there was another secret to her contentment. She never needed things to satisfy her happiness. This allowed her and Bobby to share graciously with others throughout their lives.

"You know so many young people today get on drugs and addictions because they are looking for happiness," she says, perplexed by culture changes that are so foreign to her own. "I think if they understood that happiness was inside, not outside, then they would truly be happy." She finishes with this, "It is not things that make you happy, but so often happiness is what we choose to make it."

A sandbagger in a negative context is one who misleads others about their skill set. While anyone who knows Barbara Martin would never describe her as a sandbagger, she certainly has some similar traits. Her skills and impact upon the successful life of her husband are often overlooked. While she does not get much credit, and her importance is often overshadowed, she is not concerned. Unlike the sandbagger, her intentions are not to deceive, rather she is content to allow her contributions to the successful marriage to remain unnoticed. Bobby may have never played pool, but Barbara's contentment has helped to make her husband a scratch-player in the game of life and banking.

MEANDER

There's a dying word that once thrived in the American South. When facing a similar extinction, animals are placed upon endangered lists. If words received the same treatment, then this word would indeed be protected. The word is meander. It's said more quickly in other places, but in the south it has three heavily emphasized syllables. Drawn-out with an eloquent southern dialect it's pronounced: mee-ann-derr.

Merriam-Webster defines meander as: *taking a winding path or course*. In the southern culture it's a reminder to slow-down and don't always hurry. It's not only the destination, but also the journey itself, that makes a path worth traveling. The skilled meanderer *takes time to smell the roses*.

U. S. Highway 72 runs through Walnut, Mississippi and could be described as a meander. It's the only U.S. Highway to begin and end in the same state, while traveling through two others. Heading east out of Memphis, Tennessee it takes a turn down south through Mississippi and across Alabama on its way back up north to Chattanooga, Tennessee. In other words, it meanders.

Some might ask, *why would it go through two other states to get to its destination?* To the meanderer such a question is akin to asking: *why would you peel, slice, boil and mash potatoes when you can have creamed potatoes within minutes from the box?* If you have to ask the question, then you probably won't understand the answer.

Truth is, few travel the road in its entirety from east to west. It's a beautiful scenic route that was part of the historic Lee Highway until 1926, when it became an official U. S. Highway. The entire route made a loop down south on its way from New York City to San Francisco. Rather than built as a road to get from point A to point B as quickly as possible, it was constructed with the meanderer in mind.

Another classic Mississippi saying is *out-from*. The following is an example of the proper usage for the term *out-from*. Six miles west of Walnut there is a green state-highway sign that directs travelers to turn left for Hamilton and right for Hopewell. Kids who live in the Hopewell community attend Walnut schools, and the parents go to town in Walnut. However, the parents are quick to explain that they do not live in Walnut but rather Hopewell, which is *out-from* Walnut.

For any Yankees who may be reading and a bit slow to catch-on, here's a recap. If someone tells you that they live *out-from* Hopewell, you know that you will need to *meander* several miles off of Highway 72 to get there. But you will be pleased in the journey if you are endowed with the soul of a *meanderer*.

Hopewell proper is nestled one mile north of Highway 72, at the northwest corner of Tippah County. It's near the Benton-Tippah County line on the border of Tennessee. The beautiful Hopewell Cumberland Presbyterian Church is the last remaining operational structure in the community. The church was built with wooden planks in 1843. Today, it has a white siding exterior made popular in the 1950's. At the time, the choice of this particular material was driven more by cost rather than cosmetics. But the aged look has an innocence and simplicity that makes one feel comfortable, as if they're home. Inside, the sanctuary has curved wooden pews that display the intricate details of skilled craftsmanship. From the steps of the white sanctuary you can see the remnants of a cotton gin and a country store.

In 1952, Hopewell was a thriving community. By that time, Bobby Martin was a senior in high school. He spent his summers and many a Saturday working at the gin and the store. These two establishments were owned and operated by Mr. Dan Hines. Mr. Hines was Bobby Martin's uncle by marriage, because he had married Bobby's Aunt Earlene (Valca Martin's sister).

"He's one of the best men I've ever known. I never heard him say a cuss word." Bobby says this to explain how Hines treated his employees, as well as his customers, with great respect.

Years later, Dan lost his legs when they were caught in an auger at the gin. But he never let the artificial legs slow him down physically or as a businessman. He would eventually be elected to serve in public office as the Tippah County Tax Collector.

Like Dan Hines, Bobby's brother-in-law, J. P. Coombs, was also a positive male role model for the young Bobby. Bobby describes him this way, "He had a great sense of humor and was always happy." Coombs was a successful businessman and a school teacher. As an educator, Coombs understood the value of a sound education. He also took the time to assume a father-figure role for Bobby.

One day, J. P. Coombs asked Bobby what his plans were for the future. Bobby replied in a manner that hinted to Coombs that the youngster had not given it much consideration. Besides being married to Bobby's oldest sister, J. P. was a graduate of Mississippi State University so he had affection for both Bobby and the school. Since Bobby had not invested much stock into his future, J. P. decided to take matters into his own hands and planned it for him. "You need a college education and Mississippi State is where you're gonna go."

Bobby thought this sounded like a nice idea but didn't have the money to further his education. No one in his family had ever been to college and it must have seemed as lofty as planning a trip to the moon for the country boy from rural northeast Mississippi. But Martin trusted and respected the senior Coombs, so he was willing to give college a shot. This became a life altering decision by Bobby Martin and it would likely have never occurred without J. P. Coombs' influence.

It seems prophetic that Bobby Martin grew up within a stones throw of U. S. Highway 72. Like the great road, his path to bank chairman was not so much a direct route. "I guess a person really should look out in front of where he is going, but I haven't ever done much of that." Bobby says to explain his is not the only path, or the best way for that matter.

Yet, it's the winding path that made Bobby's journey complete. Some may have gotten where they were going with a more precise plan, but none have enjoyed the journey any more than Martin. Bobby said, "I should have looked out in front of me more." The truth is, he did an excellent job of living in the now. A person doesn't make it over fifty years working at a place by only focusing on the destination or constantly wanting more.

That's one of life's contradictions. It seems by living in the now, you have the greatest impact upon your future as well. The person consumed with tomorrow has no energy for today. They will ultimately burn-out on this never-ending cycle.

Indeed, any great highway, or plan for life, needs to begin with the end in mind. However, we should not be so consumed with the destination that we fail to cherish the journey. As with most things in life, it takes balance. Bobby Martin seems to have struck that balance in a mighty concise way. As a young man, he never dreamed of one day being a bank chairman. Instead, he set goals for his life so he could reach a successful destination in whatever career he followed. But along the way he was willing to meander at times, allowing himself to smell the roses and enjoy the journey. What is the purpose of the journey if we can't find some joy in getting there? I for one, hope the word meander never dies.

HELP

Mr. Bob Smith was a member of one of the most prominent families in Tippah County in 1953. He was the proud owner of Smith's Department Store, situated on the town square in Ripley.

Mr. Smith also held the distinguished honor of being on the Institution of Higher Learning Board (IHL) for the State of Mississippi. From its inception, this has been a position appointed by the governor of the state. The IHL Board has a significant influence on the operational budget for the state's colleges and universities. Thus, the school administrators have an eager willingness to remain in the board's good graces.

Bobby Martin's uncle Dan Hines, and brother-in-law J. P. Coombs, went to visit Mr. Smith on behalf of their young protégé. After the pleasantries, J. P. Coombs got down to business. "Bob, we've come to talk to you about a boy that's about to graduate from Walnut named Bobby Martin."

Bob Smith was a smart businessman and had an idea where the conversation was leading.

"He's my wife's baby brother and a heck of a good kid. He

wants to go to school at Mississippi State but he's gonna need a little help." Coombs delivered the need as if Bobby had possessed a lifelong dream of being the first in his family to earn a college degree, sparing Mr. Smith the details that the young scholar hadn't given college much thought until his spokesman brought up the idea.

Dan Hines shared how Martin was also willing to help himself. "He works for me every summer at the cotton gin. He ain›t a bit afraid to get his hands dirty." Aversion to laziness was an essential ingredient for survival in this region of the country. Thus, being a quality employee was akin to practicing religion in this part of the Bible belt.

Coombs continued where Hines left off. "With him working for Dan, he can earn enough money to pay his tuition, but he will need a job on campus to help pay for his eats."

Smith leaned up quickly in his chair, giving a sign to his visitors that it was now his time to talk. "I think we can take care of the boy, let me make a phone call."

Bobby Martin recounts the details today as if they were a bank ledger that he had viewed just moments before in his office. "In 1953, the tuition was $218 the first semester and $200 the second. Right smart less than what it is today, huh?" he says with a knowing smile.

"We didn't have an ACT test back in those days. But we did have to pass an on-campus entrance exam to qualify." This was a daunting task for a person who had only been out of Tippah County a few times in his life and had certainly never ventured onto a college campus.

"I didn't have no real smarts, I was a 'B' student. So I was very nervous when I sat down to take the test on campus." To add to his anxiety, his name was called during the test and he was told to report to the Dean's office immediately upon completion.

"I thought, my goodness this is my first day here and I've done got kicked out already." Little did Martin know, but the dean had received a call from IHL Board member Smith and there was business to take care of. "When I got to his office, the dean told me he had gotten me a job making doughnuts in the campus bakery. He told me that I started the next morning and that I needed to be there at 4 a.m. every day."

Although Martin was concerned with his academic abilities; he had confidence in his work ethic. "I knew I wasn›t gonna be the smartest one there, but I also knew that they couldn›t out-work me."

Martin soon tired of rising before 4 a.m. each morning to make doughnuts. So, not long into the semester, he started working to impress the manager over food services. When the time was right, Bobby asked for a promotion to the cafeteria. This gave him more sleeping time since he no longer had to report for work in the wee hours of the morning. Also, part of his compensation for working in the cafeteria was that he could have all his "eats" for free. This was the first big employment decision in his life. He took a chance by leaving the donut shop and never looked back.

"Darrell Royal was the football coach and we had some real big players on the team," Martin continued in a matter-of-fact tone, "You know he's the one that went on to become legendary coach at Texas." The cafeteria was enormous and they fed much of the student body, including the athletes. "The football team had this old trainer named Dutch Letsinger. He was the meanest, cussingest thing you ever seen. He told us not to give the football players but one piece of meat on steak night. He would turn his back and they would just reach over the counter and get it themselves." With laughter intertwined, he concluded, "Then he would get mad at us when the steaks came up short, like we could control them big ol' boys."

With his summer job, he had enough funds to secure his clothes, as well as tuition. He wore khakis, white long sleeve shirts, and white buck shoes. He went home every few weeks to get his clothes washed and check on his momma. Hardly anyone in Walnut actually owned a car. In fact, only one student from all of Tippah County had a car at MSU, and it wasn't that reliable of a vehicle. Martin remembers with a snicker, "It was a rough ol' car so I didn't ever ride with him. It would run most of the time, but I could beat him back home hitchhiking."

By his junior year, Bobby had caught the eye of the student manager of the cafeteria, a job that carried with it a nice salary. The manager was a senior named Bobby McKee from Charleston, Mississippi who had been elected to Student Body President. He would go on to be a prominent eye surgeon in Arkansas, but his life was cut short when he was killed in a tragic auto accident. McKee approached Bobby Martin with a deal. "Bobby, I won't have time to manage the cafeteria and be in student government. If you'll help me, I'll be sure you get the job—year when I graduate."

The manager was also responsible for the concessions for Saturday night dances. McKee allowed Bobby to keep the revenue from this additional job and it added up to a pretty good sum. The manager kept his promise to Bobby and as a senior he was the student manager for the entire dining hall. He received a salary and all the revenue from the weekend dance concessions.

"That was my first real enjoyment with a job. I was making good money, too."

This was Bobby Martin's first experience as a supervisor of employees. His charisma served him well as a leader but he also learned how to make a positive impact upon his employers. Bobby Martin certainly gained academic knowledge in college but equally important was his maturity in personal relationships. "I think what I learned more than anything else at Mississippi State was how to get along with people. I believe learning to work with others, as much as getting your books, prepares you to be successful in life."

By the end of his senior year, Bobby had saved enough of his income to begin car shopping. It was only appropriate that the person who had been most responsible for beginning his college education would be present at the end. It was his brother-in-law, J. P. Coombs, who took Bobby to purchase his first car. The negotiated cash price on the brand new 1956 Ford Fairlane 500 was $1,750. It was equipped with a straight shift, radio, and heater. Though a modest starter vehicle, Bobby could not have been more proud if it had been the most expensive car sold in America that year. For the outlandish price of $10,430; a buyer could ride in the air conditioning luxury of another Ford Motor Company product, the Continental Mark II. But the Ford Fairlane 500 was just fine for Martin and he was beyond content. "I bet I waxed that thing 50 times. It's a wonder I didn't rub the paint off of it," Martin says with a giggle.

He and Barbara had been married a few months prior and they were ready to begin their lives together as college graduates. Though certain his hitchhiking days were behind him, Bobby didn't realize then the full magnitude of what he had accomplished. Looking back now, Martin makes a joke about his and Barbara's modest beginnings. "We left college with a brand new car and a pocket full of money. I tell Barbara we ain't had it that good since."

Bobby Martin experienced a lot of help that allowed him to earn a college degree. It was his willingness to help himself that inspired others to work on his behalf. Being a fortunate recipient inspired in him a passion to help others as well. He has a special warmth for MSU and has become one of their most philanthropic donors. But he has also expanded his generous gifts to other institutions of higher learning. It seems wherever a kid is looking for a chance to succeed, Bobby Martin is always there, willing to help.

BEST

The Two Travelers and the Farmer

A traveler came upon an old farmer hoeing in his field beside the road. Eager to rest his feet, the wanderer hailed the countryman, who seemed happy enough to straighten his back and talk for a moment.

"What sort of people live in the next town?" asked the stranger.

"What were the people like where you've come from?" replied the farmer, answering the question with another question.

"They were a bad lot. Troublemakers all, and lazy, too. The most selfish people in the world, and not a one of them to be trusted. I'm happy to be leaving the scoundrels."

"Is that so?" replied the old farmer. "Well, I'm afraid that you'll find the same sort in the next town."

Disappointed, the traveler trudged on his way, and the farmer returned to his work.

Sometime later, another stranger, coming from the same

direction, hailed the farmer, and they stopped to talk. "What sort of people live in the next town?" he asked.

"What were the people like where you've come from?" replied the farmer once again.

"They were the best people in the world. Hardworking, honest, and friendly. I'm sorry to be leaving them."

"Fear not," said the farmer. "You'll find the same sort in the next town."

Growing up in the South, Bobby Martin was surrounded by people with the gift of storytelling. Folktales like the one above have been utilized for generations to communicate wisdom.

Healthy relationships with our neighbors can sometimes be challenging and complicated. Through the lens of one set of eyes, a person or group can appear cold and dark. While to another they are seen as a ray of sunshine and warmth.

During World War II, the United States and the Soviet Union worked together in combat against Germany and the Axis Army. In the spirit of *The Two Travelers and the Farmer,* the once neighborly relationship quickly deteriorated after the war. The former allies transitioned from seeing the best in the other, to expecting the worst. This era of unrest in our nation lasted from about 1947 till 1991 and became known as the Cold War. The two countries never officially declared war upon the other, but did engage one another indirectly through combat and support of conflicts between other countries.

In the early 1950's, the Soviet Union stepped up communistic rhetoric around the world. They felt it would enhance their security to expand the foot print of communism wherever possible, while the United States was equally committed to deterring its expansion. Some historians, and understandably concerned citizens, felt that an eventual war was eminent. Both countries possessed nuclear capabilities. They began an aggressive arms race to keep pace with the other. To provide additional security and reassurance to the American people, defense areas were placed around large cities and military bases beginning in the mid 1950's. The defense area would include multiple Nike missile batteries. As many as 22 individual sites surrounded the Chicago metropolitan area alone. The Nike missiles had been designed to provide the first ever surface-to-air missile (SAM) antiaircraft. They were capable of matching the speeds of newly developed Soviet jet aircraft and could also be equipped with nuclear warheads.

The simmering relationship reached a boiling point on November 18, 1956 when the Soviet leader, Nikita Khrushchev, attended a party at the Polish embassy in Moscow. While speaking at the event, he made comments that provoked the following headlines here at home. "Raging Soviet Boss Shouts at the West: We Will Bury You."

Just a few months prior to Khrushchev's war of words, Bobby Martin had graduated from college. He understood, like many Americans, that our nation was facing a grim future in which its very existence was in jeopardy. So rather than beginning his career in business, Bobby Martin enlisted in the National Guard. He would serve for two years in active duty, from 1956 till 1958, followed by an additional five years in reserve.

"I think every able body man should serve his country for a couple of years." It seems that Martin makes this statement not out of a sense of obligation, but as an opportunity provided by our country to grow and prepare for success in life. "It really helped me to learn discipline and respect that I have carried with me my whole life."

Shortly into his tour of service, Martin studied to be a cryptographer while stationed at Fort Gordon in Augusta, Georgia. The word cryptography received its origin from the Greek work kryptós, which can be translated to mean hidden or secret. The word is used in English to define one who transmits communications in a covert manner. This was especially important during the Cold War when espionage ran rampant between the United States and Soviet governments.

Following his military education, Martin received an appointment to the Philadelphia, Pennsylvania Defense Area. There were 12 different Nike missile batteries in the Philadelphia area. Situated away from the missile launch sites were the Battery Control Areas. These facilities contained the radar and computer equipment needed to monitor aircraft in the urban areas. Martin was assigned to one such Battery Control Area on the campus of Swarthmore College, located in the Philadelphia suburbs. Martin remembers, "We were assigned to 72-hour shifts on duty. We would work, eat, sleep and get recreation all right there locked in from the outside world."

Martin is very grateful for his military experience and those who taught him valuable lessons in leadership. Not glossing over the challenges, Martin makes it clear, he experienced the good, the bad, and the ugly while in the military. "You know, I met some of the best people while I was in the service." Pausing for effect, he continues, "I also met some of the sorriest people in the world there, too." Then Martin says with a laugh, "But you know you learn something from them, too... that you don't want to be like them." It's clear that as a soldier Martin wasn't blind to the bad, it's just that he has chosen to focus more on the good.

Bobby Martin, faithful to his heritage, is a story teller and relates well to the folktale above. Like the second traveler, Bobby Martin served his country by looking for the best in her people. In the process, he has made the best out of that experience and the lessons it taught him.

I am sure that when a stranger drives into Ripley, Mississippi with the question: "What sort of people live here?" There is a good chance that the citizen will proclaim. ""We have the best." At least I'm certain such a response would come from Bobby Martin. Because he remains committed to looking for the best in the world around him.

LOANS

"The banks exposed themselves too much, they took on too much risk.... It's their fault. There's no need to blame anyone else." In 2008, Warren Buffett was the world's richest person. He delivered the previous statement about the subprime mortgage crisis that was plaguing the United States economy.

Beginning in 2001 and continuing through 2006, interest rates on financial loans were lowered dramatically to levels unseen since the 1960's. It was an effort to spur an economy that had been limping along since the dot-com bubble had deflated at the turn of the century. The result was free lending and aggressive building construction which flooded the housing market with an undervalued supply of new homes. Loans were defaulted at a high level, implementing a near economic crash throughout the nation.

Interest rates were one of the few similarities that rural Mississippi banking in 1950's shared with the free lending of the 2007 housing bubble. Aggressive lending was non-existent in the Appalachian foothills of North Mississippi during this era.

In fact, small loans (much less home loans) were hard to secure at this time and place in our history. Conservative spending was the consumer culture, as well as that of the banks.

To compensate for a modest banking industry, many local business owners extended a line of credit to their trustworthy customers. One such credit recipient was a man named Elton Wilbanks who made a living through the automobile industry in his hometown of Ripley. During tough times, he would walk around the Tippah County Courthouse Square on a monthly basis and pay back as many suppliers as possible. When funds had been exhausted for the month, he offered the remaining suppliers the explanation that they would be the first to receive payment the next month.

Perhaps the remnants of the Great Depression impacted this restriction to money borrowing during the 1950's. It was known simply as the "Depression" in this part of the country. The shortened name spoke to the emotional upheaval as well as the financial turmoil. Those who had not experienced it firsthand had certainly been well informed by the forebears of this dark time in American history. A common thought passed down from the old-timers was, "If you cain't pay for it, you don't need it."

One of the few places where large loans could be secured was with an entity known as Production Credit, whose main office was housed in Tupelo, Mississippi. However, their business model was structured to specifically support the farming industry. A loan request had to be collateralized with land before funds were issued.

After purchasing The Peoples Bank in 1950, L. E. Watson was committed to becoming one of the first banks in the region to aggressively extend personal loans. Mr. Watson had purchased and sold several banks in various locations throughout the South. He had learned that to make significant earnings in the banking industry, it was essential to specialize in loaning money.

Mr. J. K. McBride had run the bank on a daily basis since its beginning in 1925. Mr. Watson promoted Mr. McBride to Vice President shortly after purchasing the bank in 1950. This was a good choice because Mr. McBride knew the bank inside-and-out and had a good handle on the operations.

However, Mr. McBride did not have experience with conducting the level of loans that Mr. Watson was eager to begin transacting. He didn't have to look very far to find a loan officer with significant experience loaning large amounts of money.

The local manager of Production Credit was a plainspoken gentleman named Oscar Shannon. L.E. Watson saw in Shannon one who had the loan experience needed to take The Peoples Bank to the next level. Watson was able to woo Shannon away from Production Credit to be his chief loan officer. Shannon also brought along several hundred farm loans to his new place of employment.

Shannon was more than willing to embrace Watson's aggressive loan philosophy. For Shannon, this strategy was more than an opportunity to increase revenue for the bank, it also allowed him to meet vital needs in the community he loved. Instead of lending solely on land-based loans, Shannon expanded the bank's funds to meet whatever life needs existed in his hometown of Ripley. This was a groundbreaking and bold move by Shannon. "He was way outside-of-the-box of how banking was traditionally practiced in those days," says Bobby Martin. "Loans administered by banks were few and far between, but when he came on board at The Peoples Bank he started loaning to everybody." Sure, parts of his aggressive loan practices were that he saw an opportunity to make money. But perhaps more central to his motive was a passion to help the people of Tippah County.

MR. SHANNON

Although Oscar Shannon was an aggressive businessman that worked hard, at times he played even harder. He was a devout worshiper at the First Baptist Church each Sunday, but he viewed some of the church's more rigid tenants on moral vices to be "less-essential" the other six days of the week.

Prior to entering the business world, Shannon had been a schoolteacher and basketball coach. Some would say the business of loaning money is much like a competitive game. Sometimes you win, and sometimes you lose. He naturally took to the loan trade and had a skill for insuring that most notes were paid in full. Like any good coach, he had learned from experience how to guide the odds of the competition in his favor.

He was a large man with a commanding voice and personality. He had an intimidating presence that inspired his customers to *under-reach* on their loan request and *overreach* in their efforts to make their payments.

He rarely minced words and would often talk gruff to would be loan seekers. But if they hung in there, took their tongue-lashing and waited him out, he almost always delivered the loan.

A customer once asked for an amount that Mr. Shannon deemed exorbitant and he cut through the request with brutal honesty. "H*** no! I'm not giving you that loan, you'll never pay it back." On many occasions the deal making didn't begin until Mr. Shannon had proclaimed his booming verdict of, "No!"

After much back and forth the "no" eventually became a "yes" that day. Well...sort of a yes. "Give him the d*** money," Shannon uttered with disgust to his assistant. "I don't know why, 'cause he sure as h*** ain't gonna pay me back."

The loan recipient left the office a little angry and happy at the same time. But somehow this mixture of emotions stirred in the customer a desire to make certain the loan was paid in full. He had a dogged determination to prove the big man wrong for questioning his character. This, of course, was the desired result Mr. Shannon wanted, as all the theatrics had paid off once more.

The bank's current Chairman, Bobby Martin, speaks of Mr. Shannon with the highest esteem. "He could be rough around the edges at times but underneath the gruff exterior he had a heart as big as the world. He was a really great human being." Martin remembers the time a pulp-wood-cutter came into the bank in dire straits. The logger had wood shavings and grease all over his clothes. He was in the middle of a job and his saw stopped working. He didn't have the funds currently available for a replacement so he went to see Mr. Shannon. There was no mention of collateral or other vetting. The man was in need, Mr. Shannon knew he would pay it back, and delivered the needed funds instantly.

In 1958, the bank had another change in leadership. L.E. Watson was ready for retirement and sold all his bank stock to J.K. McBride and Oscar Shannon. By 1961, Mr. Shannon rose to the position of President and would successfully run the bank for the next twenty years. The bank and the community it served would never be the same. His leadership style was derived from his early days as a coach on the hardwood. He liked the underdog and relished the opportunity to make people, like his players of times past, into something better.

One of his former basketball players was a young man named Lorenzo Medford. Although Lorenzo was not yet 30 years old, he had two boys and a wife he was supporting in Memphis, Tennessee. They traveled back home to Tippah County as often as they could and needed a place to stay. He decided to purchase a mobile home to place on his family's land near Ripley. He found a modest trailer in the Memphis suburbs which he felt would work just fine for their part-time accommodations. Lorenzo made an offer to the salesman who was looking very cautiously at the country boy who wanted to write a check for the amount in full. "Son, do you have this kind of money in your account?" he asked in a demeaning tone.

"No sir, not right now, but I can make one phone call and have it there."

"Well then you better make that call before I sell you this home," the weary city dweller proclaimed matter-of-factly.

Lorenzo quickly dialed the number to The Peoples Bank. After just a moment's wait, he was put on the line with the bank's President, Oscar Shannon.

"Hey Coach, this is Lorenzo Medford." They shared a few pleasantries and Lorenzo got down to business. "Mr. Shannon, I've found a trailer that I want to buy and this feller selling it wants to make sure my check is good." Lorenzo handed the phone to the trailer salesman and said, "He wants to talk to you."

Once the phone was placed to his ear the salesman's expression began to change almost instantly. His arrogant persona started shrinking right before Lorenzo's eyes. His tone of voice became softer and he was saying over and over into the receiver, "Yes sir, yes sir…"

He placed the phone back onto its rotary base and said to the young country boy. "Son, I don't know who you are but you just bought yourself a trailer." He began shuffling the sales papers as quickly as possible in fear that the young man would leave. Maybe his most motivating concern was that Mr. Shannon would call back before he could get the sale transacted. He explained his pace with these words, "I been sellin' trailers for twenty years and I ain't never had anything like this happen." Almost white in the face, the once big shot salesman said, "He told me that he would guarantee a check from you for any amount up to $500,000."

Lorenzo Medford was not a man of great wealth. Mr. Shannon didn't even know where his former student was currently employed. But he knew what kind of man Lorenzo was and that was enough for Mr. Shannon. The $500,000 amount was an exaggeration used by Mr. Shannon to make his point. But it spoke to Lorenzo of the abundant trust his old coach had in him. "He was like a second father to me," Lorenzo remembers today.

These days, when a person thinks about The Peoples Bank, the current Chairman, Bobby Martin, quickly comes to mind. But for Martin, the legacy of the bank is symbolized in his predecessor. "He really cared for others and made us The PEOPLES Bank. He set the model for what we are today, a bank for all people."

UNITER

It's Saturday afternoon and Oscar Shannon has traded-in his business suit for farm clothes. Just hours before, he had a neck tie lying in the center of his chest. Now, he has a pack of chewin' tobacco perched there in the bib of his overalls. He walks into the general store owned by his uncle, Sam Moore, ten miles north of Ripley, in Tiplersville. The Shannon family had a farm nearby and this was where you could find Oscar most any time when he was not at the bank. He loved his work at the bank, but he had a passion for the farm.

Shannon walked into the store and saw a couple of buddies chewing the fat, standing near the crank-operated cash register. He walked over to the cheese counter and cut off a healthy hunk of sharp cheddar and grabbed a handful of crackers. After a few minutes of talking politics, Oscar changed the subject. "John, how'd your daughter do at the 4H competition?" John Shaw and his daughter had been showing cattle since the little lady had been old enough to walk. The competition was somewhat like a fancy dog show for country folk and their bovine. The stocks were bred and fed in such a way to display excellence in their breed. The Shaw's were known as having some of the most impressive cattle in the state.

"She done real good; brought home the blue ribbon."

"Dad gum, she's one heck of a cowgirl!" Shannon proclaimed. "I've got the program at Rotary next week. Why don't you come and tell the folks about y'alls bulls."

John laughed and said, "Oscar, them folks don't care nothing about our cattle."

"Yeah they do," Shannon said, objecting to Shaw's refusal. "They ain't that bad, just come do the program and you'll get a free lunch out of the deal."

Them folks, John was eluding to, were city folks. Even though all Mississippi people are seen as Southerners, there can be vast cultural differences among the various classes. Two of the more evident differences are between country folks and city people. Those most widely divided view the others with extreme caution. The country folks feel most city people are, at best, a little too big for their britches, and uppity. Some city dwellers have the same limited opinion of their country counterparts. Writing them off as backwards and lacking social graces.

John ended the conversation with a glimmer of hope for Shannon by saying, "I'll think about it."

Before leaving the store that day, Shannon had his commitment with John saying, "I'll be there but I ain't wearin' no stinkin' suit."

Shannon's gaze turned serious and he said in a deadpan tone, "That's fine, you can wear your tuxedo if you prefer."

The appointed day arrived for John Shaw's presentation before the Ripley Rotary Club. Oscar Shannon introduced his longtime friend to the Rotarians as he worked his way around the room. Shaw was not the only guest for the meeting that day. There was also a visiting minister present who had been invited to ask for the blessing upon the meal. The clergyman got carried away with his prayer and decided to pour in a considerable portion of his sermon from two days prior. When he finally finished praying and the Rotarians raised their heads from being bowed, the seat mates of Oscar Shannon realized that he had already cleaned his plate.

Shannon was always a fast eater and on this day ate right through the prayer. He consumed the meal with such vigor that his stomach worked in overdrive to digest the onslaught of food. Shannon was known by his friends as one who could pack an awful punch of gas, and on occasion chose less than appropriate settings to do so. This was about to become one of those occasions. His stomach gases kicked in with full force and started a rapid journey to the escape hatch. Unable or unwilling to hold it, Oscar relieved himself right there at the table.

It quickly became apparent to Shannon this was not a run of the mill, quiet and harmless air pocket. Instead, the fact that the expulsion of gas remained silent in no way diminished the impact upon neighboring nasal cavities.

There was no escape and Shannon knew it. He took the only course of action available to him in this circumstance. He abruptly stood, swiped the air in front of his nose and barked, "D***, John!" Then hastily moved across the room to another seat.

John was furious and would not speak to his banker friend after the meeting. A few days later, John came down with a bad cough and went to the medical clinic in Ripley. Dr. Stone was on the board of The Peoples Bank and had been present at the Rotary meeting for John's presentation. Seeing the distinguished practitioner of medicine made John mad at Shannon all over again, suspecting the physician must have thought him a country bumpkin. Instead, the humble doc greeted John like an old friend and commented on how much he had learned from his presentation. The doctor laughed with John about Shannon, enlisting him in his uncouth prank and recounted similar antics by Shannon. Before leaving, John realized Shannon had not made him the butt of a joke, instead Oscar had retained the laugh at his own expense. His city friends knew how Shannon was and had not thought lesser of John. Instead, they chalked up the event as one more story in the rich life of Oscar Shannon. Before John left, the doctor had arranged a visit to stop by the Shaw farm and inspect John's prize winning cattle.

Rather than alienating John that day, Shannon had raised-up John in the class system, by lowering himself. There was no one less refined than Shannon and he was the president of the bank. He had an innate capability of making small men feel larger, and large men feel smaller.

This was part of the interpersonal skill of Oscar Shannon. A man who united the city people and country folks of Tippah County. He was able to live in both circles and blurred the lines for each group as they looked upon the others. He was indeed a bridge builder who united his people.

HOME

Like Oscar Shannon, Bobby Martin began his career in finance with Production Credit. A gentleman by the name of C. H. Elliott was the superintendent of education in Tippah County and had a fondness for young Martin. Mr. Elliott was on the board of Production Credit and felt that Martin would be a good fit there. Bobby was asked to come interview at their home office located in Tupelo. He got the job and began his first full time employment in the professional world, loaning money in Ripley. His role involved administering and managing loans for local farmers.

After a year with Production Credit, Bobby was given an employment opportunity with Tennessee Gas and Transmission Company of Portland, Tennessee. Within a year on the job he was promoted to the position of Office Manager. Bobby and wife Barbara saw a bright future in Portland and planned on building a home in the Nashville suburb. They had purchased a lot for their home and were set to meet with a builder on the third Monday morning in May of 1961. However, Bobby received an unexpected phone call just days before, on a Friday morning.

"Hi Bobby, this is Oscar Shannon with The Peoples Bank back home in Tippah County." Martin knew Shannon as an acquaintance because Shannon and Bobby's wife Barbara were related. He also knew Shannon had done a fine job running the Production Credit office.

"Bobby we've had a tragedy in our bank. My partner, J. K. McBride, has died unexpectedly and I'm gonna need some help from someone who has experience loaning money. Would you come home and visit with me about that possibility?"

Bobby was startled by the call and didn't have time to deliberate a decision so he followed his instincts.

"Mr. Shannon, I sure am sorry to hear about this, I will certainly be praying for Mr. McBride's family and the bank. I just recently bought a home site here in Portland and plan to sign the papers with a builder on Monday."

Bobby Martin had never dealt with Oscar Shannon in business and he was about to get a taste of his persuasive skills over the phone. "I tell you what, tomorrow's Saturday, but I will be at the bank working all day. This might be a good excuse for you to come home and visit your momma in Walnut tomorrow. I'll buy your gas and eats so the trip home will be on my dime."

Bobby was surprised that Shannon didn't take his initial rejection. Truth be told, he was a bit flattered at the pursuit Mr. Shannon was giving. "Well, let me think about it, Mr. Shannon, and visit with my wife."

Shannon dug in deeper and his competitive juices were starting to flow. Perhaps he didn't realize how much he wanted the young Martin as an employee, until it looked like he couldn't have him.

"Bobby, if Barbara is there with you at home I'll just hold on the line while you talk with her a minute. I don't mean to be pushy but we need to act pretty quickly. Be sure and tell her we are not making any commitments here over the phone. All this amounts to is a free trip to North Mississippi to check on the home folks."

Bobby returned to the receiver after a few minutes and informed Mr. Shannon he would see him at the bank the next day.

Martin recalls the meeting on that spring Saturday in 1961. "Before I left the bank that Saturday I was hired."

It wasn't a lucrative salary or benefit package that lured Martin to the bank. Neither did he receive a burning bush type experience from heaven. "I was making real good money and we liked it in Portland. My salary there was $550 a month, then I had a bonus of an additional $8,000 per year. Mr. Shannon told me he was gonna start me pretty low on pay but if it worked out, he would move me up quickly."

After some prodding, Martin eventually divulged he took the job at The Peoples Bank making $350 per month. His new rate of pay was less than a third of what his annual salary had been. Trying to understand that decision now; Martin still ponders the process. "Now why did I take that job?"

Martin's faith has always been important, but he did not feel the desire to move home was a divine mandate from God. He goes on to say that several of the turns along his life's highway have not been filled with clarity. Perhaps more than anything else, the lure was in the opportunity to go home.

Today, if you ask the good church-going folk of Tippah

County if Bobby Martin was called home by God, I am sure that an overwhelming majority would answer with an emphatic, yes! These days, Bobby Martin remains a man of deep faith — trusting in his Lord to guide his steps in every decision he makes. I suspect this will remain his mode of operation for the remainder of his life. He only plans to change residents one more time, when he will be at rest in his eternal home.

FAMILY

At the end of the nineteenth century, electric streetcars were a major mode of transportation for people in urban areas throughout the United States. By 1895, there were 900 different electric railway companies serving public transit needs throughout the nation. It was into this climate that the Memphis Street Railway Company was incorporated on March 28, 1895. By 1911, the company operated 77.5 miles of track with an abundance of 310 individual cars. The electric streetcars provided more than a power based mode of transportation. The industry also became an economic engine, which impacted the city of Memphis and its surrounding areas. They offered good paying jobs that wooed numerous sons of the South to apply for work.

One such employment seeker was named Sam Moore of Tiplersville, Mississippi. He had lived his entire life in the rural farming community situated in Tippah County—just seven miles from the Tennessee State Line. Moore made the sixty-mile move to Memphis when he received a job offer from the Memphis Street Railway Company.

While the financial rewards were plentiful, Moore felt the

tug to return home to Tippah County after a few years on the job. Sam was not conscious of how much his hometown and family meant to him until they were no longer a part of his daily life. It was in moving away from the county that he was drawn back there, and would never leave the family farm again.

When Moore returned home, he had a passion to not only make a living but also improve the needs of his townsfolk. In the 1920's, he opened a general store that would service the needs of his friends and family. The store was much more than a place where individuals could buy things. It sustained life by offering food essentials and dry goods. In addition, items could be purchased on credit, which was imperative to maintaining family farms. The patrons could also procure all manner of wisdom, or at least advice, from the regulars at the checker board. To complement the store, Moore would eventually begin operating a cotton gin and feed mill as well. This further serviced the needs of the local farmers and brought more financial stability to his family.

In 1934, Sam and his wife Mary Elizabeth (known as Lizzie), gave birth to their fifth and last child, named Barbara. She would later become Barbara Martin after she and Bobby were married on December 23, 1955. Today, Barbara is not ashamed to say she was the baby and was treated accordingly. "All the family took special care of me. I probably had it a little bit easier coming up than the rest of them," Barbara says, with a mixture of gratitude and stately humility. She continues, "Financial times were much harder on my brothers and sisters growing up. But my daddy was a good business man and had done pretty well by the time I came along. We had more as a family in the later years and he spoiled me pretty good."

One of the local farms serviced by Sam Moore's general store was owned by Oscar Shannon. Moore's wife Lizzie was a sister to Oscar Shannon's mother, Effie. This officially made Sam Moore an uncle to Oscar by marriage. However, the two men would develop a bond that could not have been closer had they been blood family. It was to his Uncle Sam that Oscar reached out for help when he sought Bobby Martin for employment at The Peoples Bank in nearby Ripley. Besides being the son-in-law of one of his best friends, Oscar Shannon felt Bobby Martin would service the bank well with his experience in loaning money.

In October of 1959, Barbara's mother died suddenly of a heart attack. Just a few months after Mary Elizabeth Moore died, Barbara and Bobby gave birth to a daughter. It was fitting that they wanted to celebrate the life of Barbara's mother with a namesake, so Mary Elizabeth Martin was introduced to the world on December 23, 1959. She would be their only child.

Less than two years later, the Martin's were preparing to move home in June of 1961. Sam Moore had adjusted, as well as could be expected, after his wife's death. But the old home place still got awful lonely for him near the end of each day. It was becoming evident that after fifty years of marriage; he would never fully get over the loss of his life partner.

Since the Martin's had not made housing plans with Bobby's unexpected career change; the family moved in with Barbara's father, Sam. It's not clear, looking back now, if the family had plans to make their permanent residence with Barbara's father, or the stay just got extended. Regardless of the motive, or who initiated its implementation, the plans for a move would never materialize. The Martins would make their home in the residence of Barbara's daddy for the next fifteen years, until Mr. Sam Moore's death in 1976.

When the family talks about the decision for them to move in with Sam, it seems as though there was no decision to make. The Martin's had just started their family with Mary's birth, but it was time to bring family back home to Sam. The memories are fuzzy as if Sam invited them, or if they insisted he not be alone. It just seems their actions were built upon the long held bond of kinfolk: that is just what family does. It was this same spirit of commitment to family that inspired Sam Moore to return home to the family farm many years prior. He left behind the opportunity for a bright economic future in the streetcar industry of Memphis. He had learned long before his daughter, and son in law after him, there was a wealth back home that could not be attained elsewhere. It remains true to this day, there is nothing richer than the love of one's family.

FIRST

Prior to his death, J. K. McBride brought his son Jimmy on board at the bank. With the passing of Mr. McBride, the board elevated Oscar Shannon to President and McBride's son Jimmy became Vice President. Jimmy McBride was a people person and had a great personality, but no fault of his own, did not have significant experience loaning money. This was part of the motivation for Oscar Shannon's recruitment of Bobby Martin to the bank.

Oscar's son, Laron, remembers the date Bobby Martin began his employment at The Peoples Bank; June 1, 1961. It is etched into his mind because it was also the first day for Laron. He recounts, "I won't ever forget that day. There were so many people there, I was way out of my comfort zone." This is understandable since Laron describes himself as a bit of an introvert. His being only nineteen years old also contributed to the intimidation factor.

Laron and Bobby had never met when Oscar assembled the two in his office for a joint introduction to their new boss. That's the way Mr. Shannon worked, he was a *two birds with one stone* type person.

"I'm gonna take you boys down to meet OC. She knows more about this place than anybody else here." Shannon was speaking of OC Thomas. Mrs. Thomas had a specific role as the head bookkeeper but she also had a full understanding of the bank's complete operations. Oscar Shannon proclaimed her newest assignment to this lady of exceptional civility and intellect. "OC, I'm turnin' these boys over to you. I want you to teach 'em how to be bankers." OC treated the new employees with patience and respect. Years later, she would tease Bobby that she cried all night after that first day working with him and Laron. But like everyone she met, OC warmed up to the "boys" quickly, which grew into a deep affection for the two as the years went by.

After eight hours under OC's tutelage; Bobby asked to see Mr. Shannon regarding one more matter of business on his first day. "Mr. Shannon, I have five thousand dollars that I would like to invest in the bank."

Shannon thought this was a savvy gesture by young Martin. Establishing a savings account on his very first day of work. "Ok Bobby, go tell OC you want to set up an account and she will help you with the paper work."

Bobby corrected in a respectful manner. "No sir, I don't need a checking account; I already have one of those here. I want to buy some ownership in the bank."

Shannon was caught off guard by this proposal. It wasn't every day someone wanted to invest in the company. No employee had ever made such a proposal to Shannon, and for Martin to inquire on his first day of employment was even harder to comprehend. Although Shannon was taken aback, he was not without a response. "We don't have anyone currently wanting to sell stock, Bobby." Shannon made this statement in a slow, reflective manner as if he was in deep thought. "But I tell you what. If you believe in this bank enough to want ownership. Then I believe in you enough to sell you a portion of my stock."

Bobby and Laron worked under Mr. Shannon's leadership for 18 years until his death in 1979. Laron would have been the natural heir apparent to take over the bank's leadership. However, Laron had no desire to be the CEO or public face of the bank. He understood this shortly into his career, and just as importantly, so did his father. "He never tried to shove me into the lead role here. He was content with me being who I was." Laron says this with great affection and appreciation for his father. "I know some people would find it difficult to believe, but he was never hard on me or demanding. He just wanted me to be happy."

The casual observer might sell short Laron Shannon's impact upon the bank, but Bobby Martin does not. "He is the best business partner I could have ever had. He is sound in his decision making and has always supported me."

Laron felt that Bobby was most well equipped to follow his father as CEO of the bank. Comfortable in his own skin, Laron explains today, "I loved the behind the scenes challenges of banking. I liked working with people to help make their lives better. I didn't care for the public relations or politics that were also necessary."

This does not mean that Laron was passive or took a back seat in the bank's operations. Martin explains, "He's a great guy. If he is for you, he will get in the trenches with you. Not a bit afraid to go to battle for you, and with you, for a worthy cause."

Although Laron retired from the bank in 2002, he remains on the bank's board and continues to offer Martin nothing but unwavering loyalty. Bobby stated recently, "If I suggested to Laron that we need to burn down the bank's building, he would reply, *'Where do we need to start the fire?'*"

It takes a humble person to be willing to let another rise to the leadership role in any organization. So often we do not realize our limitations; we try to be something we are not. Still another temptation is to try to be all things to everyone. In the process, we end up being nothing to no one. Laron embraced who he was and helped Bobby excel and take the bank to unthought-of heights.

Bobby Martin purchased stock in The Peoples Bank his very first day of employment. But looking back, it seems the most important investment he made that day was in the friendship with Laron Shannon.

PHOTOGRAPHS

2020 Board of Directors:
Seated from left: Rod Colom, Laron Shannon, Bobby P. Martin, Robert W. Elliott, and Fred Moore. Standing from Left: Michael Dees, Johnnie P. Coombs, Jr., Rickey Settlemires, Kyle Smith, Mary Childs, Bob Glover, and Brian Ketchum

Mary Martin Childs, Sixth President

Bobby Martin, Fifth President

THE PEOPLES BANK

Oscar Shannon, Forth President

K. McBride, Third President

L. E. Watson, Second President

Fred B. Smith, Founder and First President

TEACHER

"Good morning, Janet, how are you today?"

"I'm alright."

"I need to visit with you after lunch, so come by my office when you have a free minute."

"Yes Ma'am, Mrs. OC."

Janet had been working at The Peoples Bank as a teller for a little over two years. One of two things was obvious to any customer that came to her window. She was either a very unhappy person or she did not like her job. In addition, Janet was often late for work, which had a negative impact upon her co-workers by hurting morale.

OC requested the meeting with Janet because she knew this problem needed to be addressed. The tempting response would have been to simply fire Janet. Her attitude was not the bank's problem to try and correct. Terminating Janet's employment and hiring someone else would have offered a quick solution. There were plenty of other people looking for work in Tippah County that would be happy to be employed at the bank. However, this was not dealing with the situation as far as OC Thomas was concerned. She cared about others and wanted to see them improve. She also believed in second chances.

So shortly after lunch, OC welcomed the young employee into her office to begin their discussion. "Janet, you don't seem very happy while you're at the bank. Do you not like working here?"

"Yeah, I like it fine."

"That's just the point, Janet. We want our employees to love working here. How can we change that for you?"

Although OC addressed the problem direct and to the point, she communicated in a very gentle manner. She was inviting Janet into the resolution process by asking questions.

"Mrs. OC, I feel like I do what y'all pay me to do. It really upset me when I didn't get moved-up to the new position I applied for a while back. That extra money could have helped my family."

"Janet, I'm gonna give you some advice and I hope you will take it. I have found that when I don't like my position in life or work, it does no good to sulk about it. In fact, a bad attitude usually makes it worse." Mrs. OC delivered this in a tone devoid of sarcasm. It was clear to Janet that she was not being attacked but mentored by Mrs. OC.

"If you think you should be making twice as much money, then how about try working twice as hard. In this way, you will make it most probable for us to give you a raise or promotion. In other words, give a level of commitment not based upon your current pay. But base your effort upon what pay and responsibility you would like."

OC was communicating a very practical approach to success that had led her to a top leadership position at the bank. She wasn't simply telling Janet what to do, but she had already modeled this principle in her own career.

"If you work like a minimum wage employee, you can be sure that this is all that you will ever receive. But if you enhance that effort, there is a good chance that your rate of pay will increase accordingly."

OC moved a little closer to Janet and softened the tone of her voice.

"Janet, the easy way to handle this would have been to have given you a layoff and say that things are slow right now. But I like you and want to see you stay here and improve for yourself and your family."

OC was not shy about sharing her affection with her employees. She did not feel this limited her skills as a manager, but rather enhanced them. Although she cared for her individual employees; she also loved the bank as an institution. Thus, she was unwilling to sacrifice the overall bank's wellbeing for Janet's deficiency.

"Janet, I'm asking for your help because I am not happy with your current performance. I want to be honest and let you know that if your attitude and effort doesn't improve, we will need to replace you here at the bank. But I sure hope it doesn't come to that."

OC delivered this news as if she was a funeral director meeting with a grieving family. She was not abrasive to her employee. Instead, she treated her like a granddaughter in need of encouragement more than criticism.

"You have two young sons that play baseball, right?"

"Yes, Ma'am."

"Did you know that if a person is batting and another player gets out trying to steal a base, then the batter gets to return to their at-bat the next inning? Not only that, but they get a new count. Even if they had two strikes the inning before; they return to the plate the next inning with no strikes and a fresh start."

Wondering where this analogy was going, Janet listened as OC made her point.

"I would love to give you a new count, a fresh start, here at the bank. You currently have two strikes but I would like to wipe that clean and begin again. What do you say, Janet, would you like to have a do-over here at the bank?" Janet became emotional and thanked Mrs. OC Thomas for not giving up on her and providing a second chance. OC embraced Janet and the meeting, or better yet lesson, was over. She was a teacher more than a boss.

Bobby Martin credits OC Thomas with having the biggest impact upon him as a manager. "She was a master at dealing with people. She could chew a person out and make them feel good about it. Now that is a true gift of leadership. She was one of the most important teachers I had in banking and life."

It was this type of leadership that propelled OC to become a trailblazer in the Mississippi banking industry. She became the first female officer at The Peoples Bank of Ripley. In addition, she was also one of the few female officers in the entire state of Mississippi in the early eighties.

When OC was nearing the end of her life, Bobby Martin had an intimate exchange with OC's daughter, Lynne Thomas Howell. OC's health had deteriorated to the point where she did not have much quality of life remaining. "Lynne, is there anything I can do to help make your mom more comfortable?"

Lynne thanked Mr. Martin for his kindness and reassured him how much he had meant to her mom. She stated there were no immediate concerns, but assured Mr. Martin she would let him know if a pressing need materialized. Looking back now, Lynne says she didn't understand initially the depth of affection that Bobby had for OC.

"When momma got sick, Mr. Martin said something to me that I had never heard before or since," Lynne shared with reverent emotions.

"You know your momma taught me how to be a banker. But the most important things she gave me was her love and patience as I learned." Such a unique statement for one professional colleague to make regarding another. It is one thing to care for co-workers, but OC exuded genuine affection and had a lasting impact.

Bobby knew little starting out in banking, and OC was there to train him. He didn't know much about the principles of management and OC was there to give a model. He didn't understand love is an important ingredient in leadership until OC demonstrated it. Before he became Chairman of one of the most successful banks in Mississippi, he began as a student, and OC Thomas was his teacher.

BEAR

As a young man, Oscar Shannon was a standout athlete. He competed as a college football player at separate stops, for both Mississippi State and Memphis State (now University of Memphis). After graduation, he became a coach and teacher for various schools throughout Tippah County. Once, a traveling fair brought along an American black bear in their caravan. It was tame, or as tame as a wild animal could be. Willing patrons of the fair were invited to wrestle the bear for a small fee. There were only a few takers as most people were more interested in being onlookers instead. As a young educator, Oscar Shannon still possessed his competitive instincts that had been fine-tuned on the college football field. So, it took little encouragement from friends and revelers for Shannon to agree to a fight with the bear. It was a lackluster affair in which the bear behaved fittingly, so that Shannon avoided injury or shame. In a nod to his wrestling partner and adventurous personality, Shannon became known by the nickname Bear from that day forward.

In the fall of 1971, Bear Shannon set his sights on a new employee to add to his pack at The Peoples Bank. "I think we need to hire that Settlemires boy from Spout Springs," he shared with his other officers.

The Settlemires boy, of which he had interest, was named Rickey. He had grown up just east of Ripley, and had gone to work at Goodyear in Corinth a few months prior. His father, Aaron, had been a customer of the bank for many years, so Oscar called the Senior Settlemires to make contact with Rickey. After a short interview process, Rickey was offered a job as a teller at the bank for the starting pay of $400 per month. Consistent with his standard mode of operation, Shannon promised Rickey if it worked out he would "take care" of Rickey and move him up in pay accordingly.

Rickey was not persuaded by the starting pay and was initially uninterested in joining the bank. But wisely, he sought the council of his father as well.

"Dad, I'm making $600 a month at Goodyear. I'm not about to go to work at the bank for $400 a month." Aaron listened patiently as Rickey made his case for the rejection.

"Son, I know it would be hard to take that big a cut in pay. But I also know that Oscar Shannon is a man of his word. If he says he will 'take care' of you, then I believe him." Rickey also knew his father felt he would have a much more secure future working with a locally owned business. Rickey was suddenly outnumbered when his future wife, Sherrell, also joined the cause for the banks' offering.

"You know what'll happen; Goodyear is going to move you to a larger city at some point," said Sherrell. She also made it clear she had no intentions of leaving Tippah County. Rickey understood this reality all too well. The only way to move up in the Goodyear corporate structure was to transition into more urban stores, which were situated miles away from rural Mississippi.

So, it was with some hesitancy that Rickey Settlemires became the newest employee of The Peoples Bank on November 15, 1971. He was appointed to the role of teller and received training from Ms. Ouida Cargile.

Just weeks into his new career, Rickey was catching on quickly. Ms. Ouida became comfortable with the progress of her young protégé and monitored his actions less closely. One afternoon, they received a visit to their teller window from one of Ouida's cousins, named Mr. Rogers. The two relatives caught up on family business, and did a bit of reminiscing while Rickey conducted the transaction. Mr. Rogers had a $100 check he wanted cashed and Rickey made quick work of the exchange. He placed five twenties into the white banking envelope and moved on to other business.

The bank had a practice of organizing the twenties in the drawers with paper clips. Five twenties would be clipped together so the tellers could quickly gather $100 worth of twenty dollar bills. In his haste and inexperience, Rickey placed five clips instead of five twenties into Mr. Rogers' envelope. So instead of giving him $100, Rickey had presented the customer with $500.

At the end of the day, Rickey began reconciling his drawer and discovered he was $400 short. He and Ouida went back over every transaction, recounted the funds multiple times, and still could not find the mistake. Finally, they made the dreaded journey to Mr. Shannon's office to deliver the news.

"He didn't say a word when we told him about the loss of $400, but I do believe he bit all the way through the cigar he had been chewing on," Rickey says looking back on the event that is transfixed in his memory, "I don't think I slept a wink that night. Mr. Rogers was at the bank as soon as it opened the next morning. He said, 'Son, I think this $400 belongs to you.'" As he tells the story, Rickey's tense demeanor transforms to an expression of joy shown by a child hitting his first home run. "I could've reached over that counter and kissed him."

Rickey quickly amended his mistake in the mind of Mr. Shannon. Within a couple of years, Rickey was being groomed as an officer. Shannon instructed him to start shadowing Bobby Martin in his daily activities. Oscar and Bobby shared the opinion it was time for young Rickey to learn the trade of loaning money. Rickey shadowed Bobby closely, but would go back to his teller window when times were slow.

Mr. Shannon observed Rickey was not staying with Bobby. "I told you to stay with Bobby and by G** I meant it! Get your a** over there and start loaning money." Rickey said from that day forward Bobby couldn't turn around without Rickey bumping into him.

Surprisingly, Mr. Shannon was harsh in this instance and soft when Rickey messed up with the $400 over payment. Maybe Shannon sensed in Rickey a shyness and lack of confidence in himself. It angered Mr. Shannon, not when Rickey made a mistake, but when he didn't believe in himself. It was through the harsh tone Mr. Shannon conveyed his confidence in Rickey.

The bear has an ambiguous nature. The Grizzly can be loud, aggressive, and dangerous when crossed. But even the largest and most powerful species can be nurturing parents. It has even been documented, adult bears will serve as foster parents when a cub is found in need or vulnerable. In addition, countless children have been drawn to the nurturing comfort of their own

Teddy bears. Rarely can one animal be characterized with such contradictory natures. Rough and gruff; soft and cuddly, all in the same body.

Bear was indeed an appropriate nickname for Oscar Shannon. Besides the name, he also shared the paradoxical nature possessed by the wild animal. At times, he could be as gruff as a mother protecting her cubs. Then others, he could be as gentle and soft as the beloved Teddy Bear. It was this honesty which drew people to him. A willingness to be who he was helped others to know he was genuine. He was indeed a bear of a man.

MOVE

When The Peoples Bank came into existence on April 23, 1925, it was located on the Tippah County Courthouse Square. With an initial cash investment of $15,000, Fred Smith was granted a charter from the State of Mississippi to begin operations as a commercial bank. Mr. Smith had his law office above the bank, and the majority of his energy was focused upon his successful legal practice.

In those early years, the institution did not extend many loans and maintained a conservative approach to banking. That changed in 1950, when L. E. Watson was sold the majority of Smith's ownership and became the bank's second President. By 1956, the bank had enjoyed healthy growth and was in need of a larger facility. Thus, they built a new structure across the square from Mr. Fred Smith's law office and relocated to 101 East Spring Street. By the 1970's, the Courthouse Square had been the heart of commerce for Tippah County for over a century. The Peoples Bank had been situated along this business epicenter for 45 of those years. But Laron Shannon and Bobby Martin shared an opinion that it was time for a big move.

The bank had outgrown yet another facility on the Tippah County Courthouse Square. The vault was too small and they were completely out of safe deposit space. All banking activity was performed on the same floor of the twenty-year-old structure. Within the work area, they had numerous mechanical check processing machines. When posting was in full gear, it sounded more like the infield of a NASCAR racetrack than a sedate financial institution. There were also no private offices in which customers could discuss loan needs in a confidential manner. The Square also presented limited parking to service the growing number of bank customers.

Bobby and Laron felt a move off the Tippah County Courthouse Square was the logical option. State Highway 15 was the main thoroughfare which connected the county and it ran through the middle of Ripley. They had visited with a nationally recognized bank construction company and it was determined a Highway 15 location would enhance their customer base. Inspired by this research, the duo began a sales pitch upon Mr. Shannon to move locations and construct a new building.

"You d*** boys!" That was the standard initial response articulated by Mr. Shannon each time the ambitious new building was discussed. Besides the financial concerns, Shannon was also receiving pressure from his neighbors on the County Square to stay put. The local store owners knew the bank's close proximity had a positive effect upon their own businesses. Shannon thought the bank was *doing just fine* at its current location, and he shuddered at the idea of upsetting his business friends.

While working on Mr. Shannon, Bobby and Laron

conducted a simultaneous sales job for the property they wanted to purchase. Hugh Clayton, a native of Ripley, was a successful attorney who lived twenty miles away in New Albany. He owned a one acre lot which was his family's old home place at the corner of East Jefferson Street and Highway 15. Mr. Clayton was an active Rotarian and would travel to Ripley every week for the meeting. Each time they saw him, the young Shannon and Martin duo would ask Clayton when he was going to sell them his property. According to their contractor, Bank Builders Inc., this was the perfect location for their new facility.

After several years of nagging, Clayton made the call one day that Martin had been eager to receive. "I think I'm about ready to sell that property to you boys. I'll be there tomorrow to talk to you." Mr. Clayton was a shrewd businessman and it was clear from the outset who would be in charge of the deliberations. "This isn't a negotiation. I will sell you my property for $100,000 on one condition. I don't want any money down. You will pay me $10,000 a year at 4% interest until paid in full."

Laron and Bobby tried to contain their excitement. "Okay, we will draw up the proper legal work." Bobby responded.

"Nope, I don't want no contract. Just set me up a note here at the bank and make the payments," Clayton said while standing. The meeting was over and a move was about to begin.

For many years to follow, Mr. Clayton loved to remind the two "boys" each time he saw them that he had gotten the best of them. "I get more fun out of telling everybody that I'm the only customer you have that you owe money to." The truth was, Martin and Shannon would have probably paid half a million dollars for the lot if Clayton had demanded it.

With their property secured, Bobby and Laron had one final

sale to close. Bank Builders Inc. had designed a 19,000 square foot two story facility. Besides the audacious size, the price tag was even more illogical to Mr. Shannon. "You d*** boys want to spend a million dollars on a building that we could put four banks in!"

Mr. Shannon was now in his sixties and knew his days as the CEO of the bank were drawing to an end. Bobby and Laron would be the leaders of the future. He ultimately warmed to the idea of the big new bank because his boys felt the move was essential for continued success. Perhaps more than anything else, his eventual acceptance of the move was a sign of support for his Lieutenants and their vision for the future.

Within a short time, the new building would prove to be a paramount decision in the prosperity of the bank. At the time of the move in 1975, the company had $25 Million in assets. That number doubled shortly after beginning operations in their new facility. By 1992, the bank had attained meteoric growth and was valued at $179 Million. Today, the bank would incur construction cost that would be four times the $1 Million price tag paid in 1975. They use every inch of the 19,000 square foot building. In recent years, they even had to expand with a new operations center.

From Mr. Smith's $15,000 in 1925, who could have ever imagined this initial investment would be the seed work for an institution that had assets in excess of $380 million in 2015? If sold today, that original investment could generate $80 million to the seller. But consistent with their commitment to serve Tippah County, there is no one at The Peoples Bank eager to sell.

The bank kept the square location open as a branch for an

additional twenty years. Persistent with their serving spirit, they eventually donated the old bank building to the Tippah County Board of Supervisors. No, The Peoples Bank will not be changing ownership any time soon. Instead, they remain committed to move Tippah County forward.

COUNTRY

In May of 1976, a college student walked into The Peoples Bank looking for summer employment. Oscar Shannon was busy, and had little interest in hiring anyone. So he made a few minutes to talk to the kid, and give him a gentle rejection.

"Hello Mr. Shannon, my name is Kyle Smith and I just finished my junior year at Ole Miss studying accounting."

Shannon was less than impressed. He was a banker and had no need for an accountant in his day-to-day operations. But Mr. Shannon saved young Smith the insult of his true feelings. "That's a mighty good degree, son, it'll serve you well in the business world."

Undeterred by Shannon's subtle lack of interest, Kyle pressed on. "Thank you, sir, I was wondering if you might need some summer help here at the bank."

Shannon ignored the subject for a moment to gather his thoughts. He then returned to the nature of Kyle's visit. "I wish I could help you, but we just hired a couple of girls for the summer and don't really need any more help right now." Shannon said, turning the kid down in a respectful manner.

"Okay, Mr. Shannon. Thank you for your time," Kyle said while standing to leave. On his way out the door, he said hello to Bobby Martin and the two visited a moment. Martin recognized the kid as the son of Becky and Joe Smith. Joe ran an iconic pharmacy named City Drug on the Square in Ripley. Martin made a beeline to Shannon's office as soon as young Smith was gone. He was eager to find out what the meeting was about.

Kyle was actually a little relieved he didn't get the job. He didn't really want to work at the bank, but went on the inquiry to satisfy a request from his mother. Smith explains, "Mom thought the bank would be a good place for me to work over the summer. I was less than motivated, but gave it a shot out of respect for her." Kyle had his heart set on working for a big accounting firm, in Memphis, after graduation. He had lived in the country all his life, and was eager to become a city dweller. He didn't see how a summer job at the bank could fit into that plan.

As soon as Kyle walked into the front door of his family's home, the phone was ringing. He answered to a growling voice on the other end of the line. "Why in the h*** didn't you tell me who you were?!"

Caught off guard by the harsh pleasantry, it took Kyle a moment to recognize the voice of Oscar Shannon. "Hi, Mr. Shannon, I thought I did tell you who I was." Kyle knew beyond a doubt that he had introduced himself, but was unwilling to challenge the big man on the details of their exchange.

"Yeah, but you didn't tell me who your momma and daddy were. They're real fine folks." Shannon said with his tone softening a bit. "When can you start to work?"

"Well, my last class is a week from yesterday. So I can start then if that's okay." Kyle said, still not exactly sure if he was being offered a job.

"Come on back to the bank when you get out of school and we'll find you something to do." The conversation ended as abruptly as it had begun. Kyle had a summer job.

"I loved it from the very first day," Kyle reminisces. "They started me at teller and I really enjoyed the interaction with so many different types of people." He shifts in his chair, responding with excitement as he recollects. "I was amazed at how the banking industry touched every other business sector in the community."

When the summer ended, Mr. Shannon offered Kyle a full-time position upon his graduation from college. The employment proposition was almost as vague as his initial hire. "I got a job for you when you get out of school if you want it," Bear Shannon proclaimed in his most enticing voice.

Although the summer internship had been a very positive experience, Kyle was still not sold on the bank. But he kept coming back, drawn there in a powerful way. He worked each time he had a break from school throughout his senior year at Ole Miss. Contrary to his ambitious goals of leaving the country life to become a big city accountant, he took the full-time job in the summer of 1977.

Kyle did not remain a teller for very long. Within one year of employment, he was promoted to the position of loan officer. Today, he is approaching forty years with the bank and he has been the institution's Chief Financial Officer for over half that time. In the late 1970's, Oscar Shannon had no need for an accountant on staff, but the banking industry has changed. Kyle now supervises a team of accountants employed by the bank to conduct their internal audit department. Smith also keeps his pulse on the daily investment status of the bank's many financial holdings.

Although his primary role is to handle the numbers, his passion remains serving the people. Kyle describes himself simply as a country banker. He still spends a vast amount of his time issuing loans and working with customers. He explains a country banker in the following way, "A country banker issues a $2.5 million line of credit to a local business first thing in the morning. Then you might help a widow lady sell some of her Walmart stock. Next, one of your customer's calls needing you to order some checks. And finally, you finish the day by issuing a loan on a 2008 Chevy Sierra pickup." Kyle ends with a big smile, "That's the best way I can define being a country banker."

While in college, Kyle Smith had dreams of being a big city accountant. His plan of getting out of the country met a sudden divergence when he fell in love with The Peoples Bank. Now, what he was trying to get away from, somehow gives him the most pride. He is indeed a country banker.

CHANGE

In 1886, an upstart technology business known as the American Arithmometer Company was founded in St. Louis, Missouri. The cutting-edge innovation they specialized in was the production of mechanical adding machines. This new invention was the brain child of William Seward Burroughs. By 1904, they had become the biggest adding machine company in America. The company's headquarters were moved to Detroit and a name change was also needed. They became known as the Burroughs Adding Machine Company to celebrate their contribution on the industrialized frontier.

They thrived for decades in the mechanical calculation of numbers. In 1953, the company made a transition into the computer industry and another name change was needed. They became known as the Burroughs Corporation and specialized their services for the banking industry. They were already capable of processing bank checks mechanically, but they saw computers as the wave of the future. Within a few years, Burroughs worked with the Federal Reserve Bank in the development of computer processing for bank checks. Change was indeed coming to the banking industry.

By the late 1970's, The Peoples Bank had made some changes of their own. They had completed the controversial move of the headquarters to a new state of the art building which was located off the county courthouse square. Oscar Shannon eventually agreed with the move, but was still no fan of change.

"Oscar, our old Burroughs check posters are just about to give out on us," Bobby Martin conveyed in a tone where he did not presume to know the solution. He only presented the problem for Mr. Shannon to digest himself.

"Yeah, Bobby, I know we're gonna need to look at getting their new model," Shannon surprisingly assessed.

"Well, that's another problem. They don't make the mechanical check processors anymore." Bobby was smart to not say the word 'computer' until asked or he felt it was absolutely necessary.

"What do you mean they don't make them anymore, they getting out of the banking business?" Shannon bristled a bit with his response.

"No sir, they've gone to computer check processing," Bobby uttered as quietly and with as few of words as possible.

"S***, they still have some old units out there, look around and see what you can find." Shannon made it clear computers were not the solution to his problem and the conversation was over.

Similar to the visionaries at Burroughs, Laron Shannon and Bobby Martin understood the need to transition the bank into the computer age. However, Mr. Shannon was in his late sixties and unwilling to embrace the technological change. Out of respect for Oscar, Bobby wouldn't argue with the senior Shannon on the subject. Laron felt it was necessary for him to be the one to push his father in this uncomfortable process.

After months searching, Bobby found a couple of options for replacement mechanical check processing machines. The problem was the offerings were used models of an antiquated product. Besides their inefficiency, there was concern with finding replacement parts for machines that were no longer in production.

Laron made one final push with his father. "Are you sure you don't want to upgrade to the computerized posting machines?"

"I am," Mr. Shannon answered in a definitive tone. "The mechanical processors have always done the job. I'm not ready to change."

"Well if you won't upgrade to computers; will you do a lease, instead of a purchase, on the old processors?" A defeated Laron relented.

This set Mr. Shannon's blood boiling, he had heard enough. "I'm sick of talking about this; when I'm gone you boys can get the biggest d*** computer that this oversized bank building will hold."

However, the very next day, Mr. Shannon agreed to allow the bank to begin computerizing in the accounting department. The old Burroughs mechanical check processors would become a thing of the past. Mr. Shannon never grew to trust computers, but he did believe in his officer's vision for the future. It was that trust in his people that inspired Mr. Shannon to embrace the change that was necessary.

A few weeks later, Laron and his father were working on the family farm mending a fence. "You know, son, its gettin' time we start thinking about selling this farm." Mr. Shannon was getting older and spending more time at the bank and less at the farm.

"Granddaddy would turn over in his grave if you sold this farm. We can't do that."

Mr. Shannon continued working the claw hammer against the old wooden fence post. Someone had long ago placed tin vegetable cans on top of the post to inhibit rain from pounding the top of the wood as it aged. It was unclear if the can labels had been removed prior to installation. They all looked alike now; a copper shade that city people were beginning to pay big money to achieve. They were calling the aged look patina, but country folk still called it rust. Mr. Shannon gave a simple reply, "I think Granddaddy would understand, son. Let's go get a coke." He ended the conversation as he wiped the sweat from his now wrinkled brow.

Within a year of this day on the farm, Oscar Shannon would die unexpectedly. Laron suspects now his father was preparing him for a change himself. "I don't think he ever intended on selling the farm as long as he was alive. It brought him too much joy." Laron says with his voice becoming even softer than his customary quite cadence. "I believe he had that discussion about selling the farm that day to prepare me for what I would have to do after he was gone. I think it was his way of letting me know it was okay to one day sell the farm."

The Burroughs Corporation has remained in business with a variety of different names and business models since 1897. It was their willingness to change while maintaining their principles which has allowed them to survive. Laron led his daddy to make the necessary changes to keep The Peoples Bank in existence as well. I think Laron's suspicions about the farm were correct. Mr. Shannon may not have liked change but he understood it was necessary in life. So, his talk that day about selling the farm was not for himself, but for Laron. In business and in family, both father and son were preparing the other for the change that was indeed to come.

JHA

In 1976, Jack Henry and Jerry Hall devised an innovation in banking. They created an off-the-shelf computer software package specific to the industry. Their strategy focused upon being a technology partner for small, community banks.

It was an unremarkable beginning for Jack Henry and Associates, as they generated a meager $9,360 in revenue for the year 1976. But besides providing cutting edge technology, they also focused relentlessly upon customer service. The entrepreneurs were willing to adjust their core system to meet the specific needs of their users. This was a game changer for the success of Jack Henry and Associates. With this commitment to serving the customer's requests, they inspired a multitude of banks to accept them as their single point of contact for bank information processing.

As a result, Jack Henry and Associates exploded with meteoric growth. The company went public on October 29, 1985, eventually becoming a Standard & Poor's 400 Stock Market Index. Today, the company describes itself thusly, "We now serve as the primary technology partner for more than 1,300 banks ranging from community banks to multi-billion dollar mid-tier banks and multi-bank holding companies." They are now a billion-dollar company with more than 6,000 employees in 40 locations.

But back in 1980, Jack Henry and Associates was just gaining a foothold in the community banking industry. When time permitted, Mr. Jack Henry would personally call on banks that were good prospects for his innovation. He heard that there was a growing bank in Northeast Mississippi ready to embrace the computer age. So in 1980, Mr. Jack Henry made a cold-call trip to The Peoples Bank of Ripley, Mississippi.

Bank Chairman Bobby Martin remembers the visit by Mr. Henry well. "He sat right there in my office," Martin says while pointing across the bank lobby to what was once his work station. "He had on a pair of blue jeans and a white short-sleeve dress shirt."

The Peoples Bank had ceased mechanically processing checks, but were depending upon a larger company to handle their computer processing. Mr. Henry shared how the bank could use his software to conduct their own computer-based check processing. "Every request we made of him, Mr. Henry complied right there that day," remembers Regina Morton, Vice President and Information Systems Manager. "No matter what the software tweak was that we asked for, his answer was 'yes' every time." This was no accident, or sales-job by Jack Henry. His company was built upon an eagerness to adapt their software to meet the meticulous needs of the community banks.

In addition to creating distinct software design on the front-end, Jack Henry and Associates continues to provide excellent customer service anytime problems arise. Regina Morton further explains, "If you have an issue and your computers are down, it can be catastrophic in our industry." Pausing to reflect objectively, she continues, "I don't think we've ever had a time when we were down to exceed 30 minutes. JHA always gets right on the problem."

As a Senior Vice President and Marketing and Personnel Manager, Becky Benson has long had an appreciation for quality communication. Thus, she points out that another value of JHA is their commitment to being user friendly. "They communicate in language that bankers can understand, and not a lot of computer jargon."

Twenty years after making the plunge into computer check processing, The Peoples Bank became the first bank in Mississippi to implement electronic check imaging. Today, when banks distribute statements to their customers, there is a photo copy (or electronic image) of all the checks processed for the month. Prior to this change in technology, banks would mail the actual processed checks back to the customers.

But when The Peoples Bank became the trailblazer for electronic check imaging, they didn't force-feed-it to their customers. Becky Benson explains that the bank hosted various customer forums to explain the change. They also continued to deliver both, the traditional checks as well as the new electronic images for a time-period. However, they still had a handful of customers that never did take to the electronic check imaging. Therefore, the bank continued to process checks by traditional means for those customers wary of the electronic images. Benson shares the motive, "We were not going to lose any customers over this advance in technology."

This is what sets apart companies like The Peoples Bank

from their competitors. They are always looking to the future, while keeping one eye on the past. Perhaps it would be better to say that one eye is always on the customer. The bank realizes that their past, and any hope for a future, is built upon the customer. As they embrace technology and cutting edge innovation, they never lose sight of its purpose. They understand that the primary role of improved technology is to better serve the customer, not the company. In other words, the goal of The Peoples Bank leadership is not to make their jobs easier, but to constantly embrace their motto of *making banking a pleasure*.

Like The Peoples Bank, Jack Henry and Associates was founded in a town of less than 10,000 people named Monet, Missouri. They have maintained the headquarters there for more than forty years, along with a commitment to serving the other, not self. In his book, *You don't know Jack...Or Jerry: From Small Town Roots to Financial Software Giant*, Robert O. Babcock shares the story of Jack Henry and his business partner Jerry Hall. He describes the two as Missouri country boys who never forgot from where they came. "The Golden Rule—treat others as you would want to be treated—is engrained in both of them, and that applies to their employees, their customers, their business partners, and their suppliers."

It's no wonder that these two entities that began with small town roots continue to share in partnership to this day. It's their common commitment to excellence that draws them to one another. The tools of their trade require innovation, but the real secret to their success is built upon these timeless principles: hard work, clear communication, and relentless customer service.

Bobby Martin concludes his thoughts on Jack Henry and

Associates with this nugget, "So many companies today try to sell you on their products. Jack Henry and Associates doesn't hope you buy what they are selling. They adjust what they are selling to meet what you are buying." Martin pauses for effect, "There's a difference, you know."

Indeed there is, Mr. Martin.

LIGHT

Laron Shannon walked briskly toward his car that was parked on the outer limits of the bank's lot. The rain had just begun and was making a momentary splatter upon the canvas of his white shirt. Laron was unaware when he placed a black tie around his neck that morning of how it would symbolize the day's event. It was 5:00 PM on Monday, September 10, 1979. The rain had begun, but the storm was still to come.

He pulled out of the bank just as Lloyd McCluskey was pulling in. McCluskey flagged-down Laron and got out of his car, mindless of the increasing rain. Laron subconsciously knew this was not a social visit. Lloyd had driven to the bank instead of calling, and the news was too important to deliver from the comfort of the automobile. He walked across the rain soaked parking lot and went to Laron.

This dreary day was the polar opposite of the energy on display at the bank just two days prior. It was on that Saturday that Laron's parents departed Ripley for their annual trip to Las Vegas. Before leaving town, Oscar had come to the bank for a few minutes. He was exceptionally jovial and made an effort to speak to everyone on the main floor. This included customers and bank personnel alike. He was dressed fittingly for a trip to the city in the sand. He had a resemblance to a modern day Al Capone, clad in a pin striped suit and his favorite wool felt dress fedora perched up top. He was giddy about the trip and an opportunity to get away for a few days from the pressures of banking. Oscar certainly loved being with his customers, but even the most energetic social butterflies need to get away at times.

The personal attention to banking extended beyond the walls of the institution into his home. Laron Shannon remembers, "Momma never knew who daddy would bring home for lunch on a daily basis. If he was talking to a customer near lunch time, he would invite them to come eat." Though she would fuss at Oscar a bit for the surprise visitor, she had a passion for serving others. Mrs. Bessie Shannon was one of the best piano players to ever tickle the keys at the First Baptist Church in Ripley. As a staunch Southern Baptist, she had no affection for the gambling made possible with their yearly visit to Las Vegas. However, Mrs. Bessie did enjoy the entertainment shows and could sometimes be persuaded to drop a coin, or two, into a slot machine. She avowed that whatever winnings she received would go to the church. *Heaven knows, the devil had possessed that money long enough,* she reasoned.

Like his wife, it was something beyond gambling that drew Oscar to Las Vegas each year. He was in no way a high roller, and set strict limits upon his gambling budget before arriving. It seems the greater draw to this place is captured more fittingly by one of its numerous nicknames: the *City of Lights*. The energy and entertainment found there was a symbol of his personality. He was flashy, loud, and full of life. He had energy and enthusiasm for living life to its fullest. Las Vegas was not so much a place, but a kindred spirit to Oscar.

His son Laron explains, "You know, dad's health was not good throughout much of his adult life. He had severe diabetes and high blood pressure. I think he lived longer than he ever thought he would." His approach to life resembled that of baseball legend, Mickey Mantle, who once said, 'If I knew I was going to live this long, I'd have taken better care of myself.' The younger Shannon continues, "I think that is why he lived life so much to the fullest, because he knew that each day could be his last."

It was with this awareness that Laron Shannon was met by Lloyd McCluskey in the bank parking lot that fall day of 1979. McCluskey's parents had made the trip with Oscar and Bessie so Laron suspected that this visit was likely bad news. Lloyd shared with his friend in the empty bank parking lot that Oscar Shannon had just died of a massive heart attack in Las Vegas. The sprinkling which had begun minutes prior had now intensified. It was dark, and the rain poured.

It took several days to get the body home from Las Vegas. The weather continued to be dreary, and the sun had not shined upon Tippah County since Oscar Shannon had died. The rain continued all the way until the day of the funeral. The water was so overwhelming it crossed highway 15 in front of the bank and made the highway impassable. It was the most water some old timers could remember falling at once.

But before the funeral was over, the rain stopped. As the day ended, the people of Tippah County saw something they had not witnessed since Shannon's death. The sky began to show signs of light. It was a subtle, symbolic reminder; the darkness would not last forever.

On the Saturday before his death, Oscar Shannon departed his bank for the last time. As he neared the exit, he paused for a moment and removed his hat and used it to give a wave to his staff. "I'll see you boys next week," Shannon said before crossing over the threshold.

When he joined the bank in the 1950's, he ignited a spark of hope for his community. By 1979, he had aged aggressively, along with the bank. Besides a few strands of hair brushed front to back; his head was now mostly bald. This created a shine on the top of his crown that emanated from a light source above. As Shannon exited the bank the light continued to shine within the institution. Although he did not return to the bank the next week as promised, his legacy of light and love will live on in Tippah County forever.

LEADER

It's 6AM on a fall morning in 1979. The barbershop pole has just been ignited and is beginning its slow spin. The red, white, and blue stripes present an optical illusion in which they appear to be moving down the pole, rather than around it.

The regulars come in just as the percolator coffee maker begins its gentle groan. The standard conversation piece is politics. Although local events take precedence over the national spotlight, there is often a limited supply of small town news. The discussion of politics will never materialize on this day because there's a hot local news topic on the streets of Ripley. Ralph pours a cup of coffee and hasn't taken his first sip before he broaches the subject. "John, I seen you at the funeral yesterday. What'd you think about the service?" Ralph was a skilled tactician when it came to barbershop talk. He knew how to bait the others into expressing their opinions without being quoted on the streets himself.

"They done a good job. He was a heck of a man!" John said, adding a bit more to the celebration of life for Oscar Shannon.

Bob picked up on John's comment and guided the

conversation in the direction Ralph was hoping when he introduced the subject matter. "I tell you one thing, that bank is in big trouble now."

Ralph, still cautious not to form his own opinion, stirred the pot a little thicker. "Well, if the bank is in trouble, then we're all in trouble."

This made Bob a little more anxious and more eager to share his concern. "There ain't no way them boys can run that bank the way that Mr. Shannon did."

John, the diplomat, added some hope. "Bobby Martin's been the President for a while now, you don't think he can handle it."

Bob took a step back and fed off John's more relaxed tone. "Look, I know Bobby Martin is a good guy, but he ain't no Oscar Shannon. How can you replace somebody like that?"

Ralph took a chance to bring out more derogatory opinions by entering others into the subject matter. "They might put Laron or Jimmy McBride in charge and pass-over Bobby."

The barber spoke for the first time and, as always, was careful to limit his comments to the facts and not speculation. "Laron don't want it. He told me himself that he never has wanted to run the bank. He loves the bank but he ain't married to it."

Bob was back, unconcerned with any semblance of a filter of what he was thinking. "I wish Jimmy McBride would take over, 'cause I like him better than any of em. But Jimmy don't even live here anymore, and he may not want to move back to run the bank."

Ralph ended the conversation by saying what they all already knew, "I'm not sure what's gonna happen, but I think the bank is gonna sink or swim with Bobby Martin. He's the man now."

Jimmy McBride was the son of Oscar Shannon's business

partner from years prior, J. K. McBride. Much like Oscar Shannon's death had left a void in the banks leadership, J. K. McBride's sudden death in the early sixties presented the same vacancy at the bank. Jimmy McBride, like Laron Shannon, had grown up with the bank. Neither heirs had indicated to Oscar Shannon an interest in leading the bank. So, it was to Bobby Martin who Shannon directed his energy in grooming a successor.

Oscar Shannon appointed Bobby Martin as the bank's president in 1973. He had worked side by side with Shannon since coming on board in 1961. Shannon had experienced being thrown into the sole leadership role at J. K. McBride's sudden death. He wanted to insure his successor was prepared before his departure. Martin was prepared and knew the business inside-out, the only question that remained was could he lead the bank in Shannon's absence.

Bobby explains, "I utilized what Oscar had taught me about banking, but perhaps more importantly, I tried to model his leadership style." Shannon's strong personality never left any doubt who was in charge. Martin embraced this same style, and it became clear quickly that he would be a leader others would follow.

Within two years, Jimmy McBride was no longer an employee of the bank. He sold his stock to Bobby Martin and left the bank on good terms. This was a brave decision by Jimmy McBride. He realized that the bank had too many chiefs and one needed to go. It is a reflection on the character of Bobby and Jimmy that they came to an amicable business separation. We can learn from this lesson in leadership from Bobby Martin and Jimmy McBride. They knew that a change needed to be made and did not avoid the discussion. Instead, they addressed the challenge in as delicate a manner as possible. This is what it means to truly be a leader. Firm on principles and the health of the institution, but administering those tough decisions in as gentle a way as possible.

The barbershop gang walked into their club the first morning after Oscar Shannon's funeral filled with pessimism. As they looked upon the pole, with its downward spinning stripes, it served as a symbol for their outlook for The Peoples Bank's future. However, while some barbershop poles present an illusion that the stripes are moving downward, others turn in the other direction and the movement goes upward. Similarly, the barbershop talk regarding The Peoples Bank did not remain negative for very long after Oscar Shannon's death. It became clear early on that the bank, in Oscar Shannon's absence, would continue to move like the latter pole, upward and not downwards. Unlike the barbershop pole, the northerly movement was not an illusion. The bank would not go backwards or even maintain in the years to come. Because of Oscar Shannon's grooming of a future leader named Bobby Martin, the bank was able to continue on the path of success that Shannon began long ago. Upward and outward was the movement of the bank, then and now. They continue to be a community and industry leader that would make Oscar Shannon proud.

COTTON

"Without firing a gun, without drawing a sword, should they make war on us, we could bring the whole world to our feet... What would happen if no cotton was furnished for three years?... England would topple headlong and carry the whole civilized world with her save the South. No, you dare not to make war on cotton. No power on the earth dares to make war upon it. Cotton is King."

This statement was delivered by Senator James Henry Hammond of South Carolina in 1858. Tensions were mounting between the North and South, but Hammond used this logic to argue a Civil War would never materialize between the States. History would prove the senator wrong. Demand for cotton was strong, but its influence was not such to dissuade the coming conflict. When powerful people become entrenched with vastly different ideologies, war can become imminent.

In response to the Civil War, United States cotton production suffered a setback. To fill the void in the worldwide demand, cotton production increased rapidly in Egypt and India. Once slavery was abolished in the wake of the Civil War, sharecropping evolved to compensate the labor needs for Southern cotton farmers. Landless blacks and whites were employed to work the crop for a share in the profits of the landowner. This model of operation helped Southern farmers regain their foothold as the world leader in the plant's production. Cotton remained on the upswing until the mid-twentieth century. It was then that cotton's dominance in the clothing industry suffered from the development of synthetic fibers, most notably polyester. Thus, the economic engine was no longer churning out the profit margins which had inspired its nickname a hundred years prior: King Cotton.

But cotton was not dead, and by the 1970's, it once again made an economic resurgence. Cotton has indeed had an up and down journey on the financial landscape of the Deep South. But pressing on past every challenger, it remains the bestselling fiber in the United States today. Thus, it still holds an important role in the financial market of our country. It has even surpassed its limited role as a commodity used in clothes production. It comes as a surprise to some that the main ingredient for currency bills in the United States is not paper, but rather cotton.

It was the good cotton prices of the 1970's that inspired Fred Moore of Tiplersville, Mississippi to pour the majority of his farming operations into cotton. Fred had joined his father, Sam Moore, in the agricultural industry many years prior. Besides farming, they had also operated a successful store, cotton gin, and feed mill in this community located ten miles north of Ripley. But by the early seventies, they had concentrated all their efforts into farming.

Their main cash crop was cotton. They planted a few acres in corn as well, to feed livestock. But they made their living in cotton. Most farmers practice a necessity known as crop rotation. The Moore's implemented this strategy of alternating the crop planted on a specific piece of land. In other words, although the more fertile ground was primarily used for cotton growth, sometimes they planted corn there in its place. This practice replenished the soil of nutrients which had been depleted from cotton growth. This also enhanced soil fertility and crop yield.

Although they had a systematic process to determine crop rotation; the formula was not an exact science as Fred explains, "You didn't want to rotate too often, because you wanted your best land planted in cotton." Then Moore adds with a knowing laugh, "You sure didn't want to rotate when cotton prices were good."

Shortly after the Board of Directors for The Peoples Bank made Bobby Martin their Chairman in 1979, his brother-in-law, Fred Moore, was also added to their number. Besides being the brother of Bobby's wife Barbara, Fred was also related to Martin's predecessor, Oscar Shannon. Moore's mother was a sister to Shannon's mother, making the two men first cousins. But Fred Moore's selection as a board member was not an unmerited family favor. The Moore family had amassed a strong holding in the bank's stock and it was fitting for them to gain a voice on the Board of Directors.

Fred Moore brought good old-fashioned horse-sense and wisdom to the Board of Directors for The Peoples Bank. His gentle counsel served as encouragement to the bank's leadership from the very beginning. His thirty-five years of service make him the longest tenured board member who is not an employee of the bank. Moore learned from the leadership style of strong board members that preceded his time at the bank. He fondly remembers a beloved local physician's guidance, "Dr. Stone was always supportive of the bank's CEO. He believed in helping the person you employed to run the bank." Moore embraced this same style. In his mind, *it is not the board's job to micro-manage the work of their leader, but assist them to do their work most efficiently*.

While some boards are much more active in the daily operations of the institution they serve, this has not been the practice of The Peoples Bank. They approach it from the point of view, *if the person you have hired is making you money, then leave him alone and let him do his job*. It's hard to argue with this standard mode of operation performed by The Peoples Bank board. They have made a profit every year for their entire ninety-year history.

Besides currency being manufactured from cotton, there is another connection between the fabric and banking. Just as Moore learned early in his farming career, you don't want to rotate crops when the cotton is plentiful. He and the board have applied the same principle to managing the bank's leadership. Wise bank boards, like farmers, don't want to change their strategy when their efforts are producing a high yield. Since money is made of cotton, it can be said Bobby Martin has maintained high cotton prices at The Peoples Bank. Thus, the board has had no desire to rotate his leadership for over thirty-five years as the board's chair.

GOLDEN

Becky Benson started her employment at The Peoples Bank in 1980. She was a fifteen-year-old high school student when family friend, OC Thomas, offered her a job. "Mrs. OC asked me to help with filing after school and in the summers," Becky remembers.

A few years later, Becky spent time working with a nationwide bank while in college. But as soon as possible, she returned to The Peoples Bank where she remains an employee to this day. "I really gained an appreciation for the community bank after I worked in a big corporate structured institution."

Now, 36 years later, Becky has worn many hats at the bank. Today, she is a Senior Vice President with responsibilities over Marketing and Personnel. She keeps an employee handbook in the top drawer of her desk. It's a sound document devised by various employees that make up the personnel committee. Becky turns to it frequently when confronted with problems. She wants to make sure she is consistent in dealing with all her employees. "Mrs. OC always told me if you treat everyone the same, they will respect you," she says with her affection for OC

Thomas still radiating. "They may not always like your decision, but they will respect it, if you are fair and follow the rules."

Like Becky, Justin Thompson joined the bank just after finishing college on April 1, 2000. Justin had been working at the bank only a short time before some of the female employees took a special interest in his needs. His most pressing need, in their minds, was for Justin to find a wife. On one occasion, Bettye Harrell called Justin from her desk across the bank. "There's a cute girl over here, you need to come *check out*. You don't have to say anything, but just stop by my desk for a minute." Mrs. Eugenia Parson worked near Bettye and had not been made aware of the covert plans instituted by Justin and Bettye to simply "check-out" the unsuspecting customer. When Justin entered Bettye's work station, Eugenia stopped him in his tracks. "Justin, you might want to meet this nice girl, her name is Jenny."

Justin was caught off guard by Mrs. Eugenia's take-charge tactic. He was also more than a little embarrassed. Since Mrs. Eugenia had handled the introductions, there wasn't much else for the young couple to discuss. They smiled politely and went on about their business. However, a spark must have ignited in the not-so coincidental meeting, because within a year Justin and his new-found acquaintance would be engaged.

Eugenia was taking Justin under her wing and looking after his needs. Treating him like she would have had he been her own son. In helping Justin in the dating process, Eugenia was doing what OC Thomas had done before her. Twenty years prior, OC had introduced Becky Benson to the rules of the bank. Now Eugenia was doing the same thing for Justin. OC went by a printed book while Eugenia's was unwritten. In spite of being transmitted by different means, the rules were rooted in the same message. Treat others the way you want to be treated. They were practicing the Golden Rule.

Eugenia worked at The Peoples Bank for 42 years until her sudden death in an automobile accident on June 1, 2014, at the age of 77. This was devastating to the entire bank community, because she was like a grandmother to many of her co-workers. As an employee, she started working at the bank because of what she received there. But her enduring legacy is rooted in what she contributed to others.

A male co-worker once asked her teasingly, "Mrs. Eugenia, I heard a song the other day that said, *'Women get prettier at closing time.'* What do you think that means?"

Mrs. Eugenia had never visited a bar at any time, much less closing time. "I don't know why they would say that," she said while subconsciously fixing her hair. "You think they would say they look better first thing in the morning, instead of at the end of the day."

Eugenia worked well into her golden years. When most people would want to be home with their grandchildren; Eugenia became a grandmother to her coworkers at The Peoples Bank. Eugenia felt no need to retire early because her golden years were made better by the practice of the Golden Rule. In the process, she has inspired a new generation of dedicated women who have made a long career at the bank. Regina Morton, Paula Windham, and Carolyn Street have all surpassed thirty-five years of service. Joining this list is Becky Benson who is on her 36th year of service. To this day, Becky still turns to her rule book in dealing with a tough decision, thinking of the women who have gone before her, each time she does. Remembering the greatest rules OC and Eugenia taught her were the golden ones.

HUMBLE

David Horton joined The Peoples Bank in 1982. Prior to that, he had been in banking for ten years at a neighboring institution, known as the Bank of Falkner. At one time, the Bank of Falkner had been larger than The Peoples Bank, but the latter had surged past its competitor by the time of Horton's transition.

Falkner is a small town located six miles north of Ripley. The town of Falkner was named for Colonel William C. Falkner who was a resident of Ripley in the late nineteenth century. He became known by some as the "Old Colonel," because of his rank and service in the Civil War. He was also a successful lawyer, businessman, and author. He was elected to the Mississippi Legislature in 1897, but was shot and killed by a former business partner shortly thereafter. Today he is most well known as the great-grandfather of the Noble Prize winning author William Faulkner.

Residents from the town of Falkner are quick to point out it was young William who messed up the spelling. Local historians believe the famed author added the "u" to his family name prior to becoming a literary icon. It was part of a ploy to pose as an Englishman, in an effort to join the Royal Air Force.

The town of Falkner has not seen its population of three hundred change much since the days of its birth on the Appalachian frontier. When the soft spoken David Horton came to work at the Bank of Falkner in 1972, he fit in well with the rural setting whose residents valued hard work and humility. His customers appreciated this, although Horton gained success as a banker, he never became too big for his britches.

David's mom, Lillie, was a sister to Barbara Martin. Although Bobby never aggressively recruited his nephew by marriage; he always let David know the door was open for a job at The Peoples Bank if he ever wanted it. Finally, after gaining ten years of experience at the Bank of Falkner he was ready to make the move.

Horton's first role, after joining The Peoples Bank, was to manage the construction of a new north branch located in Ripley. He also assisted with the establishment of an upgraded computer processing system for the bank. David will tell you he helped with the new branch and computer system because he didn't have very many customers at the start. Thus, he had more time than the rest of the officers to dedicate to these time sensitive projects. While there is some truth to this humble assessment by Horton, there was likely a deeper reason for his diverse responsibilities. Bobby Martin knew from the beginning, David had the wit to catch-on quickly and excel on multiple levels. He is one of those rare, brilliant individuals that can do almost anything. His intellect is sometimes camouflaged with an "aweshucks," farm boy demeanor. But anyone who has ever worked with Horton will tell you this unassuming nature is quite contrary to his unsurpassed IQ.

In 1992, The Peoples Bank established their first branch

beyond the city of Ripley. It would be located near the northernmost limits of Tippah County, in Bobby Martin's hometown of Walnut. The Peoples Bank had possessed a cooperative working relationship with the Bank of Walnut for several years. They began electronically processing the banking transactions for the Walnut bank in the late eighties. The Bank of Walnut eventually asked for, and accepted, a purchase offer from The Peoples Bank.

When the buyout was finalized, David Horton was selected as the manager for the new location. Little did David, or his uncle, know that the building experience with the north branch would serve him well for future needs at the bank. As the manager of the Walnut Branch, he was called-on to oversee construction of the new facility. David had some apprehension about making the move from the main office to the Walnut Branch. Most of all, the humble banker was overwhelmed with the awesome responsibility of running the operations for an entire facility.

In more recent years, a young man named Curtis made a stop by the Walnut branch one day seeking a loan. He had his eyes on a brand new Ford F-150 Lariat, four wheeled drive pickup truck. After being rejected by other loan agencies, Curtis suspected the meeting would be quick (he had learned it doesn't take long to say 'no'). But he had an extra few minutes and thought he would give The Peoples Bank a try since they had a location in his hometown of Walnut. Besides, if they said 'yes' it would be well worth his time.

When Curtis walked into the loan officer's private setting he was surprised. David Horton greeted him with a big smile and looked more like an elementary school principal than a Senior

Vice President and Branch Manager of a 300 million dollar bank.

By then, Horton had gotten over his initial concerns of moving to the Walnut branch and was in his comfort zone. "It's been good to work this close to home, and help out so many folks that I know," Horton explains. But on the day Curtis came seeking a loan to buy a truck, it seemed that David would be unable to help. David had to be the bearer of bad news to the would-be pickup buyer, Curtis. However, sometimes the help we need is not the same as what we want.

"We're not gonna be able to issue a loan, with your current credit score," David delivered the news with the compassion of a surgeon lamenting an inoperable brain tumor.

Curtis's suspicions had been affirmed and he would not be receiving a loan from The Peoples Bank. But in addition to the "no," he received a strong dose of financial advice. The loan seeker explained he had several bills and he just couldn't keep his head above water.

David had heard similar accounts numerous times over his more than thirty years at the bank. He offered a plan which he had shared with many in the same boat. "Why don't you start working to pay off the smallest note that you have? Once you get that one out of the way, you can move on to the next one." David explained that human nature is to want to pay off the note with the highest interest rate. However, those are sometimes the very loans in which the most money is owed. By starting with the smallest loan, regardless of the rate, you can attain some success and then move along with confidence.

The loan seeker, Curtis, listened to the wise counsel, but it did not fully sink-in. He was still thinking about the truck, more than the financial woes that got him into this predicament. "So, you think I need to wait on the truck for a little while?" Curtis asked.

David responded, "Why don't you get a vehicle that you don't have to add on another big load of debt to buy." He continued without being abrasive in his tone. Far from it, his posture remained pastoral. "How about thinking about your financial trouble a little every day. Don't wait until you need to make a purchase to be concerned about your credit. If you will do that, then you can get this thing cleaned up, and you can put your financial woes behind you."

David Horton gains a great deal of satisfaction in administering advice, which if followed, will help people out of financial peril. It not only helps financially but also brings more balance and happiness to every part of their life.

David Horton was hesitant when he was initially called upon to lead the Walnut branch. Many people of faith are familiar with Moses having a similar hesitancy when he was called upon to lead the people of Israel. The Sacred Scriptures would later describe Moses as the most humble man to ever walk upon the earth. Horton would shudder with a comparison to Moses, consistent with the banker's humble nature. He may not be a Moses but he has indeed embraced the humble nature that allowed Moses to have a positive effect upon so many. Like Moses before him, Horton eventually warmed to his leadership role in a strange new land. In the process, he has helped many people with his humble approach to leadership.

COMMUNITY

In the early 1990's, OC Thomas began laying out plans for her retirement from the bank. She had been an employee since 1953, serving as Vice President of Operations for more than ten of those years. Some people have the capacity to retire from a job and never look back. But then there are those, like OC, that become emotionally attached to their occupation. More than a job, the bank was where OC practiced her livelihood. She gained, she gave, she led, and she lived through the bank. It was time to retire, but just cutting ties and walking out the door on her last day was not an option. It was with this attitude she paid the bank President, Bobby Martin, a private visit one afternoon.

"Bobby, it's getting time for us to start planning my retirement from the bank." He listened patiently as she laid out her plans.

"I think we need to go ahead and secure a replacement, and allow me to work with them for about a year." There was no argument here from Bobby. OC was the one who had trained him how to be a banker and refined his leadership skills. He respected her opinion about her future, much as he had trusted her with his own journey.

"Now, you know who we need to hire to fill my role," She felt that Bobby's daughter, Mary, would be the perfect fit.

But Bobby expressed his uncertainty "I don't know if she would come."

"Well you won't ever know if you don't ask her," OC stated with a dogged determination.

Bobby agreed with his banking mentor and said, "Okay, I'll talk to her." OC had done much of the talking, and Bobby had listened patiently. But as the conversation drew to an end, Bobby had something to say. "OC, I want to thank you for all you have done for this bank. And there's no way I could ever pay you back for all you have given to me personally."

"Go get your daughter from that bank in Tupelo, and that will be payment enough."

Mary was serving as Operations Officer for the Corinth, Mississippi facilities of BancorpSouth. In 1987, The Bank of Mississippi in Tupelo merged with First Mississippi National Bank to become BancorpSouth. The institution is well-respected throughout the South, and is a major player in the region's banking industry.

So, it was with the motivation of her predecessor that Mary came home to The Peoples Bank in 1990. She was a single mom at the time, having gone through a divorce just a year prior. Her son Bob had been born on May 19, 1983 and she received significant help from her parents in his upbringing. "Bob stayed with Nanny from his birth, I don't know what I would have done without her and dad."

Mary's transition to leadership at The Peoples Bank was a

natural fit. She began her career at the Bank of Mississippi, because she wanted to make it on her own. Mary explains, "I felt it was important for me to start at another banking institution. Looking back, it probably would have worked out fine if I had started here at The Peoples Bank." She gained valuable experience at the Bank of Mississippi by also going through their intensive management program. She concludes, "I am grateful for what I learned at the Bank of Mississippi."

Mary had grown up with the bank. She witnessed the countless hours her father poured into the institution. Back in her high school days, she was a cheerleader at Walnut. Her mother never missed a game, but Bobby was frequently absent because of community events representing the bank. She understood the personal demands and was not sure if she wanted to take her own family down the same route. She considered the prospect of going into veterinary medicine, but ultimately her heart could not say *no* to banking. Sure, she experienced the times her dad could not always be there solely for her family. But she also witnessed firsthand the way he dedicated himself to help the people of his community. Ultimately, it seems she could not escape the desire for helping people which had been instilled by her daddy.

In her twenty-five years with the bank, she has seen the industry continue to change. But she remains committed to the way Peoples has conducted banking for over ninety years. "I think there will always be a place for the community bank." Mary describes a community bank as one which is impassioned about providing quality service to their customers. She explains, "If a customer calls looking for a referral to another professional service, we don't simply give them a name. We also look up the number for them." When you go to a community bank, you don't have to search for a specialist in their company. They do the leg work instead, and take out as much red-tape as possible for their customers.

In addition to serving the customer inside the bank, the community bank is also committed to impacting people outside the bank as well. The Peoples Bank has become the leader in philanthropic and charitable work throughout Tippah County. In the process, they have become the gold standard of what it means to be a community bank.

To enhance the spirit of joy found in giving, they have implemented a process of providing employees a set number of days each month to perform charitable work. The employees are compensated for their community work with pay from the bank. Mary explains this motivation in the following way, "When people do something for someone else it makes them feel good. Not only are we improving the community, but we are also improving the lives of our employees by providing them this opportunity to serve others outside of work."

The Peoples Bank is committed to wanting what is best for their community in every aspect of life. In the process, they are building a greater sense of community among their employees and enhancing morale on a daily basis. They are indeed a community bank.

RETURN

Shortly after Mary Childs came home to work at The Peoples Bank, they implemented their first ever credit card program. Also, this made possible the convenience of ATM banking for their customers. As Operations Manager, Childs provided oversight to the company's transition into the world of plastic money while Bettye Harrell provided management of the day-to-day credit card activity.

Harrell began her career on January 2, 1976 as a secretary for the bank's officers. However, she put her career on hold from 1983 till 1990 so she could spend time raising her children.

Bettye Harrell was not the first to return to the bank after a hiatus. Joe Griffin served the bank from 1967 until 1971 before leaving for a career in sales. He came back to the bank in 1987 to serve as a loan officer.

The credit card operations required Harrell and Childs to attend annual conferences, and Joe Griffin sometimes joined them in their travels. On one occasion, they booked air travel for a lengthy trip. As the three sat together on the jet, Joe was given the window seat. The weather was rather stormy and the pilot announced they were going through the edges of a storm cell. He instructed the passengers to remain in their seats, with their belts fastened, until they reached smooth air again. Joe had extensive flying experience and felt more like they were right on top of a thunderstorm, rather than between weather cells.

Suddenly, a fire ball ignited from the wing. It was just outside of Joe's window. The ladies asked him abruptly what happened. It took a moment for him to process, but after a brief pause he shared his suspicion. "We've been struck by lightning." Joe tried to reassure the girls everything was going to be alright. Truthfully, he remained uncertain until the jetliner's wheels touched safely down.

Bettye Harrell is a lovely person inside and out. She takes great pride in her appearance and how she treats others. Joe has a hearty sense of humor, and occasionally reminds her of the lightning strike. "Bettye, when that lightning struck, your hair stood straight up on your head." Joe continues with a big grin, "I think I saw smoke coming from your head the rest of the day."

On another trip, the trio traveled to St. Louis, Missouri for seminar training. While there, they were able to take in a visit to the acclaimed St. Louis Zoo. They made their way past a cage belonging to gorillas. The silverback male took a special interest in Bettye. Like his cousin King Kong, the gorilla had a warm spot in his heart for lovely ladies. He began banging a trash can and looking directly at Bettye. Regardless if his intentions were peaceful or destructive, Bettye didn't wait around to interrogate. Later, when separated from the girls, Joe returned to the gorilla for another visit. He maintains the ape appeared to be heartbroken. Upon closer inspection Joe was sure he saw a tear running down its rugged face.

When Joe left the bank for greener pastures in 1971, he had no visions of one day returning. Now, he enjoys his work so much there he never wants to leave. Understandably, Bettye took a few years off to raise her family. But after that season in her life she, like Joe, felt a pull to return to her banking family. Although Mary never left the bank as an employee, she had grown up with the bank. When she eventually joined the bank. it was like a coming home for her as well.

Mary, Bettye, and Joe have indeed had some memorable travel experiences throughout the years. But no matter how much fun a trip provided, they were always ready to return home by the week's end. Likewise, it was professional detours away from the bank that made them cherish returning there to work. And because they did return, their lives have been improved and so has The Peoples Bank and the customers they serve.

RESPECT

By 1992, The Peoples Bank had risen to become the 19th largest bank in the state of Mississippi, with assets totaling $178,901,822. This was a meteoric rise from assets which totaled $15,600,000; just twenty years prior.

They had expanded operations to three branches in the city of Ripley, and would soon add additional branches throughout Tippah County. The bank purchased a company car to transport documents between its various branches. Tempted by the allure of the new car smell, Mr. Martin had made a habit of driving the car home for lunch. However on one occasion, Mr. Martin had to go out of town for the day so the car was still at the bank when Kyle Smith's lunch hour approached. Being a senior officer at the bank, Smith decided to drive the car home for lunch on this particular day, in Mr. Martin's stead.

After a brief lunch, Kyle went back outside and climbed into the bank car. As he turned the ignition, there was an explosion and smoke instantly poured from under the hood. While an expert in financial matters, Kyle had very little knowledge of the inner workings of an automobile. Although a novice with all things mechanical, Kyle knew enough to deduce the car would not be up for a return voyage to the bank. Despite being just a month old, the bank car had made its last mile. When Kyle returned to the bank in a different vehicle; his coworkers suspected that something was wrong. With an expression as though he had seen a ghost, he delivered the grim news of the cars untimely demise.

Mr. Martin was not expected back at the bank that day, and would not arrive home until later in the evening. Regardless of the late hour, Kyle drove his personal car to Mr. Martin's home to await his arrival. This was news Kyle wanted to deliver in person, and he didn't want to wait until the next morning.

When asked about the wait, Kyle answers he just thought it was the right thing to do. But as Kyle describes Mr. Martin's nature, a deeper answer evolves. "He has that innate leadership quality that commands respect from others."

A few weeks later, Bobby Martin was making one of his regular walks throughout the main floor of the banking lobby. As he approached, one of the officers subconsciously straightened his neck tie. At the same moment, a teller sat up a little straighter while another began organizing her work station.

This was a particularly slow day for banking. Martin moved toward the window of one of his tellers whose eyes were getting a little heavy on this long day. Martin offered a sneaking smile while creeping up to the counter. He raised his right index finger to his lips, surprising the staff with his quickness toward the window. He suddenly slapped the counter and the young teller's eyes burst open. She saw Martin and horror came over her face. She responded immediately with an adamant defense. "I wasn't asleep!" Martin got a big laugh out of the exchange and grabbed both hands of his employee with a warm embrace. He said very calmly, "How's your heart, Susie?" He then let out another chuckle.

It seems all of these behaviors are related. The officer straightening his tie, the teller's response, and Kyle's long wait for Martin's arrival home; they are all rooted in respect. Some people seek to lead an institution by a hard charging demeanor and distance themselves from their employees. What they create is fear rather than respect. This may be a way to lead, but it does not embody leadership. Martin's staff is not fearful for what he will do, but rather grateful for what he has already done. Respect is not so much something that is demanded, rather it is commanded. Respect cannot be forced; it must be earned.

When asked if he sees a connection, Smith says, "Without a doubt!" Kyle remains an expert of financial matters rather than automotive mechanics. But even someone with his skill finds it hard to conceive the bank's consistent growth. He ponders the following, "It may be Bobby's leadership skills as much as his banking knowledge that has driven us forward?" Smith says this with affection and admiration in his voice. The tone of one eager to make many more miles with Martin behind the wheel of the bank's car.

RELATIONS

The school bus driver stopped at an uncharacteristic location from the neighborhoods he normally visited. A young boy exits the bus and runs into The Peoples Bank. Once inside, he walks unannounced into the office of the banks CEO, Bobby Martin. Martin is on the phone when the young man enters. The child has an innate instinct to sit quietly until the conversation is completed. The youngster begins punching the numbers on the adding machine which is placed purposefully on the executive's desk. When Martin finishes with the call, he directs his attention to his guest, "Hello, Mr. Bob, how are you today?" He says while extending his right hand.

The youngster stands, grasps Martin's hand firmly, and begins shaking hands. He says with a big smile "I'm doing good BePaw. How are you?"

The shake continues for ten seconds. Martin stares deep into the child's eyes. Bob looks back with the same intensity. He is unwilling to be the first to look away. As the greeting comes to an end, Martin says to the kid, "That's a mighty good handshake, good to meet you Mr. Bob." Bob is the ten-year-old grandson of Bobby Martin and he is practicing an art that his grandfather learned when he was Bob's age.

As a youngster growing up in Walnut, Bobby knew a well-dressed businessman from the community named Jewel Rowland. He remembers seeing the classy looking man downtown on one occasion in particular. The adult wanted to shake hands with Bobby so the youngster sheepishly complied. Bobby looked down and gave him a limp fish of a handshake. Rowland said with energy, "Boy, let me show you how to shake hands." As a big smile came across his face. "You stand up straight, look 'em deep in the eyes, give a firm handshake, and grin like a mule eatin' briars."

Today, Bobby remembers this exchange like it happened just yesterday. He says, "You know that was an invaluable lesson that I've taught to countless young people myself," Martin says, emphasizing the importance of making a good first impression upon another. He expands on the lesson taught by Mr. Rowland by saying, "You know, you meet somebody with your eyes, your mouth, and your hands," he says explaining the importance of good eye contact, a nice smile, and a firm handshake.

So by the time Bob Glover is ten years old, he has been well schooled in the art of handshaking. As the only grandchild of Bobby Martin, he will grow up with Martin and the bank central in his life. It would seem natural for Bob to one day join the family business. However, his career aspirations will change several times throughout his childhood. By middle school, Bob was working on the family cattle farm after school and on Saturdays. He showed cattle competitively and learned the value of hard work as a cattleman. At this age, Bob hoped to eventually trade in the farm tools for surgical instruments and become a medical doctor.

By high school, he had set his sights upon becoming an architect rather than a physician. Glover explains today, "I liked the creative expression of architecture and the structure it offered." But Bob made a keen observation while on campus for a Mississippi State football game one Saturday. He discloses, "I noticed while many students were headed to the game, the engineers and architects were still studying." Bob gives a hearty laugh and reveals his chief motivator for career change. "That School of Architecture parking lot was filled with student's cars, even on ballgame weekends."

Glover started attending the Mississippi Bankers Association Annual Convention when he was just a kid and developed lasting friendships. "I have always had a knack for numbers, and I loved the relational aspect of banking." So, by the time Glover enrolled in college at Mississippi State University, he had decided to pursue a career in banking. "Although I liked math and was intrigued by the banking industry, I still was not convinced that my future would be at The Peoples Bank." Glover flirted with the idea of moving to an urban area and becoming an investment banker. His family never put pressure on him to join The Peoples Bank, and continue their legacy in banking.

During college, he started working at the bank on school breaks and gained a deeper appreciation for the connectional nature of the community bank. Glover explains, "Ultimately, it was the relational aspect of the hometown bank, and the opportunity to work with family that drew me to a career at The Peoples Bank." It seems many of Glover's decisions in life have revolved around relationships. He shares personally, "So much of what we do in life hinges on our relationships. Whether its faith, family, or work, a healthy life is built upon healthy relationships."

It is evident that Bobby Martin has taught his grandson, Bob, much more than how to shake hands. He has impressed upon him the importance of good relationships. In addition, he emphasized that good relationships begin with good introductions. The old saying is true, *You never get a second chance to make a great first impression.*

SWEET

On a spring day in 1994, Bobby Martin gathered members of his staff at the bank's headquarters for an important announcement. "I think everybody that works here would agree that I'm a rat." After hearing the shock of this statement, the banking leader then asked a question, "Now, do you want to help make me the Biggest Rat in Town?"

His challenge was spurred on by a nationwide fundraising campaign orchestrated by The American Cancer Society. The organization would visit large towns or small cities and ask well-known local civic leaders to engage in a competition. The participant who could generate the most support to fight cancer would become known as the "Biggest Rat in Town." The charity explained, while rats are traditionally seen as pest; they play an important role in the fight against cancer. With that in mind, competitors could count it an honor to be known by the American Cancer Society as the "Biggest Rat in Town."

Bobby Martin embraced the challenge with vigor. He was highly motivated to assist the charity with this endeavor. True to form and Martin's passion for community service, he was ultimately crowned The Biggest Rat in Town.

The Peoples Bank staff continued the campaign for several years and the funds grew so large they felt a need to expand their giving beyond the American Cancer Society. A new fundraising campaign was birthed known as "50's Day." The bank continued giving to the American Cancer Society, but also expanded their donations to local charities.

The 50's Day theme was the creation of two officers of the bank, Roger Childs and Ronny Ketchum. It embraced the music, fashion, and pop culture of the 1950's era in American history. In addition, it was also a play on the word "fifty." The bank has a daylong celebration complete with a carnival type atmosphere on the bank's grounds. Food and other items are all sold for fifty cents. Since its inception, the day long charitable event has continued to gain success. The institution has generated at least twenty thousand dollars a year for the past ten years. The bank underwrites the costs and donates 100% of all revenue to charity.

While the 50's Day has contributed a wealth of resources to local charities, the amount is only one-tenth of the annual giving shared by The Peoples Bank. Bobby Martin is hesitant to disclose the exact amounts of his personal giving partnered with the bank. However, it is believed by those close to him the combined philanthropic giving to date is well into the eight figures.

These days Roger Childs is still a busy man at the bank. It seems anytime you call upon him, he has several projects going at once. He is a Vice President with over twenty years of service at the bank. Roger Childs spends much of his time at the bank committed to community efforts on behalf of the company. It may seem strange to some that a bank would use the skills of a trained loan officer to oversee various giving operations. However, at Peoples they believe what they contribute to the community is just as important as what they receive. Therefore, Childs's efforts not only concentrate on bringing in funds to the bank, but also dispersing them with the same precision.

He is a longtime member of Spout Springs Presbyterian Church. While some people remember the exact time and place of their conversion to faith, Child's journey is different. He officially joined the church by making a profession of faith when he was twelve years old, but he never remembers a time when he was not a believer in Christ. He has been surrounded by the faith and church since birth. Spout Springs is a country church in which most all the worshippers are related. While many children of the church have moved on to urban worship communities, Roger has stayed put in the place where it all began for his faith journey.

The worship service is very simple and informal. Roger explains, "We have just a few hymns that we sing on a regular basis because our pianist is not very well accomplished." Childs makes this assertion and then replies with his customary hearty laugh. "I'm the only one who can poke fun at the musician, because I'm the one who plays the piano."

Roger is also a skilled baker and can offer up some of the best desserts you've ever tasted. This is one more way in which he uses his talents to bring enjoyment to others. He understands that the sweets he serves up don't meet all the recipient's dietary needs. It's the meat and potatoes that sustain life, but the sweets oftentimes make life worth living. Besides adding pleasure to one's taste buds, the sugary treats also communicate warmth and affection in ways that words cannot.

Roger's primary professional role is to provide loans and generate revenue for the bank. Loans are the meat and potatoes of the banking industry, the life blood of the institution. But like serving up secret dessert recipes, Roger also enjoys his charitable work the bank allows him to gift to the community. It doesn't provide the sustaining food that fuels the bank, but it does bring a little more joy to the life of those to whom he presents the gifts. Roger was nurtured by the love of his church family as a child. This prompted in him a desire to share a similar affection with others. It is in receiving that The Peoples Bank has been inspired to give as well. Roger Childs is pleased to be part of their giving by adding a little sweetness to their customers and community.

EDUCATION

In 1995, Larry Robbins was the Superintendent of Education for the South Tippah School District. Ripley High School was the largest school in the district, and in need of additional classroom space to accommodate their growing student body. Robbins and his board had the desire to construct a Math & Science Complex on the campus of Ripley High School. The new building would serve two purposes upon completion. The need for additional classrooms would be addressed. In addition, the state of the art facility would enhance education in the critical areas of math and science.

The total price tag for the new building was projected to be approximately $1 million. The school district held a promise of matching funds from the State of Mississippi in the amount of $500,000. Supporters campaigned feverishly before the citizens of Tippah County for a bond measure to supply the additional $500,000. A bond works somewhat like a loan for government entities. The Peoples Bank of Ripley was willing to be the bond holder and had agreed to charge the school district a minuscule amount of interest for the borrowed funds.

Although more people voted in favor of the bond than

against it; a 60% majority was required for passage. When the bond failed to receive the required number of votes; Robbins traveled to the state capital in Jackson, Mississippi to weigh his options. He was given an additional six weeks to raise the matching funds. After that time period, the availability of state funds totaling $500,000 would expire.

From 1969 to 1991, Robbins was the principal at a local school named Blue Mountain. While serving as the school's chief administrator for 22 years, he somehow found time to teach and coach basketball as well. He was a coach and leader at heart. This helped the Cougars from Blue Mountain boast some impressive teams during Robbins' tenure. Now, just two years into his job as the Superintendent for the school district, he was faced with a test unlike any he had ever endured on a basketball court.

Robbins returned home to deliver the grizzly news to his board and the active supporters of the project. Despite the challenge, Robbins made it clear he was not ready to throw in the towel. Kyle Smith and Rickey Settlemires of The Peoples Bank were inspired by Robbins' passion and assisted with a plan to retain the matching funds offered by the state.

Rickey Settlemires explains, "We established a group called the 'Bakers Dozen' tabbed with recruiting area leaders to contribute one thousand dollars each to the campaign." Superintendent Robbins orchestrated the strategy with the precision of a game plan devised from his coaching days. "We met every week and would go down the phone list. Each member of the 'Bakers Dozen' gathered a list of names to call over the next week. We kept going until we had all the funds raised," Settlemires remembers.

In addition to giving effort to the "Baker's Dozen," the boys from The Peoples Bank complimented the campaign with an additional strategy. After collaborating with the bank's CEO, Bobby Martin, they presented the Superintendent with an idea. "What if we approach some of our willing customers with a plan to draft $83.33 from their bank account each month for one year?" Settlemires reasoned. Robbins loved the idea and was grateful for the bank's willingness to implement the strategy for their customers.

"I can't even remember how many of those bank drafts that we setup, but it certainly inspired more participation," Kyle Smith says, downplaying the fact that the bank received no interest or reimbursement for this service.

Larry Robbins had a dream that the Math & Science Complex could be built with private support. The assistance provided by The Peoples Bank and the generosity of many citizens of Tippah County helped to turn Robbins' dream into a reality.

A few years after the building had been completed, Larry Robbins had this to say in a newspaper interview with the Tupelo Daily Journal (now the Northeast Mississippi Daily Journal). "This community, if they believe in what you're trying to do, money's no object." Robbins provided more details of the urgency needed to raise the funds within the six-week time period or lose the matching funds from the State. "We started that night…within a week, I had $200,000 in the bank. In the bank! We raised a total of $425,000 for the Math & Science Project."

Robbins had learned what many others had also experienced. When The Peoples Bank gets behind a project for their community; failure is not an option. The bond measure failed to receive the number of votes needed to pass. This inspired in the community a different kind of bond. A commitment by concerned citizens who bonded together on behalf of education.

WELLNESS

In 1996, the sport of racquetball came to Ripley with the construction of the Tippah County Hospital's Wellness Center. It seemed as though everyone in Ripley wanted to tryout this new fad. With interest so high, it was difficult for players to secure a time on the courts. Since Bobby Martin was already accustomed to waking at 4:30AM each morning, he decided to incorporate 5:00AM games to beat the rush. He encouraged his grandson, Bob Glover, and a maintenance worker from The Peoples Bank named Edward Gray to join him.

When three people play a game of racquetball it's called *cutthroat*. In *cutthroat*, the server competes against the other two players in an effort to gain a point. Since two against one makes scoring difficult, the name *cutthroat* seems appropriate.

The Wellness Center was built to complement the hospitals traditional *sick-care* with a *prevention* model of healthcare. The Peoples Bank of Ripley embraced this new wellness concept of the Tippah County Hospital. In addition to promoting better health for their employees, the bank also saw the benefit for the entire county. So much so, they pledged $150,000 to contribute ongoing support of the Wellness Center.

Shortly after one of his very first racquetball games, Bobby Martin met with a 23-year-old man seeking a loan to purchase his first home. The loan seekers name was Patrick, and he had very little credit history since he was just entering the workforce. He remembers today, "No one else would take a chance on me." So without even an account at The Peoples Bank, he set an appointment with Mr. Martin.

Mr. Martin knew Patrick's family well, and the young man had a good name in the community. They shared in a bit of small talk and then Mr. Martin said, "Let's go look at the house." After driving up to the house, Martin saw no need to go inside for further inspection. When they returned to the bank, Martin looked the young man in the eyes and asked, "Can you make the payments?"

He answered without hesitation, "Yes sir, I can."

Martin got out of Patrick's older model Ford car and cheerfully ended the meeting, "Okay, write a check—it's yours."

Patrick remembers every detail from that day, "You never forget something like that. He helped me when no one else would."

Today, Patrick's partnership with The Peoples Bank reaches far beyond his own home. Patrick has grown up to have a successful career in the medical industry and is now the CEO of the Tippah County Hospital.

Recently, the Wellness Center was in need of a new floor. The rubber flooring that best fit their specifications came with a $60,000 price tag. Fortunately, the manufacturer was WARCO BILTRITE, who has a facility located in Ripley. The manufacturer had graciously agreed to sell the flooring at half price. While $30,000 was a wonderful price, the hospital only had an

$18,000 budget for the replacement. So it was with dread, Dr. Chapman explained to his board that they would have to delay the floor replacement. When Mr. Martin got word that the floor was still over budget, he reached out to his old friend Patrick Chapman. Mr. Martin offered for the bank to split the $30,000 cost with the hospital. WARCO BILTRITE was so moved by the bank's generosity that they decreased the floor cost by an additional $6,000.

This cycle of generosity began because WARCO BILTRITE was willing to assist their local hospital. The Peoples Bank was inspired by WARCO BILTRITE's willingness to help and wanted to partner with the floor manufacturer. In healthcare, the wellness strategy may prevent illness, but the partnership that made it possible for a new floor is indeed contagious.

You never know if the young person that you take a chance on today will one day become one of your most valued customers. This is not a call for us to manipulate others in our favor. Instead, it's a model of treating others the way we want to be treated.

Bobby Martin still frequents the hospital's Wellness Center regularly with Bob Glover and Edward Gray. For the skilled *cutthroat* player, the strategy is clear. Seek out your opponents weakness, capitalize on their vulnerabilities, and you will win. However, the wellness approach to healthcare is just the opposite. You help another person overcome their weakness rather than taking advantage of their vulnerability. In this model, you both win. The Peoples Bank and the Tippah County Hospital are indeed committed to working together for the Wellness of their community.

THEATRE

Kathy Voyles has served as the pianist for the First Baptist Church of Ripley since 1976. She works the instrument with the poise of a teenager operating a smart phone. Kathy has been a performer since the age of seven. "When I was a kid I loved the piano; the larger the crowd the better I played."

As she grew older, Voyles had a desire to help others develop a passion for the fine arts. She would eventually earn a Master's degree in Speech and Theater. She became an educator in the public school system by teaching Elementary Gifted Music and High School Chorus in Blue Mountain, Mississippi. She also became active in community theatre which offers people of all ages opportunities to perform. She explains her motives in this way, "The arts provide a wholesome way for people to express themselves, because not everyone plays ball. Sports are great, but many need another venue to grow in a fulfilling way."

By 2003, Voyles had a dream of establishing a performing arts center in Tippah County. She set her sights on a building that was once the home of a local movie house known as the Dixie Theater. The family of attorney Griffin Ladner had possession of the old building and graciously granted the property to the City of Ripley for use as a live performing arts center. The City established an entity known as *The Theatre Guild* and asked Voyles to take on the leadership role.

The Dixie was in need of extensive renovations to make it performance ready. Voyles secured a $160,000 grant from the Mississippi Arts Commission, but had to match it with $110,000 raised locally. The Theatre Guild hosted a gala and multiple dinner theaters. They also sought private donations and assistance from area businesses. In addition, she asked several donors to give $1,000 each to make a significant impact on the renovations.

One of those she visited seeking the $1,000 contribution was her longtime friend, Bobby Martin, at The Peoples Bank. She shared how when she embraced entertainment it gave her confidence and the people skills needed to succeed in life. She helped Martin see her vision of inspiring a similar opportunity for others in their community. She revealed her vision for creating a top level local theatre, and her need for some additional financial assistance to create the program.

Martin listened politely to her plan of securing $1,000 donations from multiple local businesses. He paused the conversation by placing his hands behind his head, stretching back in his chair, and looking beyond Voyles. He was thinking, and Voyles' mind raced as she wondered if his were good thoughts or bad. "I think we can help you," Martin began. As Voyles thanked him with the thought of a $1,000 gift, Martin continued as if he didn't hear her expression of gratitude. "If you can get ten people to contribute $1,000 then the bank will match it with an additional $10,000."

Bobby Martin believes business and economic development is heavily impacted by impressive and talkative people. "At some point in life you're gonna have to sell yourself to get the job you want. If all things are equal; people are going to do business with who they like." In addition to enhancing personal skills, Martin believes that the arts can have a positive effect upon an entire community. He speaks glowingly of the theatre's impact upon Tippah County. "I think our investment in the Theatre has been one of the most successful partnerships for the bank and the community." To date, The Peoples Bank's contributions to the local theatre has reached six figures.

"It provides a place where people can come together from various backgrounds throughout the community." Martin explains with amusement. "Some people performing on the stage had never even been to a play before they acted in one."

Trying to understand why the bank would invest so heavily into the theatre takes a deeper look. Besides developing teamwork and leadership skills, the theatre offers culture and entertainment on a local level. "People come from the surrounding areas and can't believe that we have such high-level productions right here in Ripley," Martins says with certainty.

As with all investments made by The Peoples Bank, the theatre has an economic impact as well. "People realize that they don't have to go to a big city to experience quality entertainment. They can spend their money right here at home and impact their community," Bobby Martin explains.

These days, Kathy Voyles still strolls to the piano with a confidence of the seasoned professional that she is. With the assistance of The Peoples Bank and the Dixie Theatre, she is helping other people experience this same passion. Along the way, gaining confidence for themselves and pouring strength into the community for which they perform.

BMC

Blue Mountain College was founded in 1873 by Civil War Brigadier General Mark Perrin Lowrey as a college for young women. The College webpage describes its beginning this way, "As a village preacher before the war, General Lowrey was a man of vision who saw the importance of providing a thorough education for women. The General felt that the South's recovery would be enhanced by the educating of its young women."

It became a world class institution for women studying in the field of education. Not only did the women gain careers and enhance their local economy, but they also had a reciprocal effect upon this entire region of the nation by positively impacting the children that they would educate.

In 1956, at the request of the Mississippi Baptist Convention, the College opened its doors to men preparing for church-related vocations. The College's passion for expanding their reach into the community and impact upon the world continued to grow. On October 4, 2005, the Board of Trustees of Blue Mountain College unanimously voted to make all programs offered by the College available to male students, thus making BMC fully co-educational. The Chair of the Board of Trustees for the school was Bobby Martin from The Peoples Bank. He had this to say on the historic occasion in the life of the College, "Opening all programs to male students at Blue Mountain College is evidence of the institution's commitment to serve students who desire to study in a Christian environment."

Today, the school is privately owned by the Mississippi Baptist Convention but maintains tuition rates that more closely resemble public school costs. Thus, their ministry is not only educating students with a Christian world view, but they do so with a low cost tuition. In annual ranking of U.S. News and World Reports, Blue Mountain College is consistently ranked as the number one Best Value of Regional Colleges in the South.

One goal of the school is to improve the number of college graduates in a state hungry for economic growth. According to the U.S. Census Bureau's 2014 American Community Survey, Mississippi had the lowest average household income of any state, at $39,680. Some attribute this trend of lower incomes as a direct correlation to the relatively low number of citizens pursuing higher education. Just 21.1% of adults in Mississippi had a bachelor's degree as of 2014, versus the national attainment rate of 30.1%.

In addition to educational excellence, the school is one of the top employers for Tippah County. Therefore, besides improving the local work force by education; the school also has a direct positive impact upon the local economy by the jobs it creates. Few are aware that the College has a faculty and staff payroll of more than 100 people. This equates to a lot of good paying jobs for the hard-working people of North Mississippi. When you consider the ripple effect from college wages, benefits, institutional spending, and student spending, the total annual impact is in excess of $20 million on the local economy. Thus, the College serves as an economic engine, on multiple levels, for the people of Tippah County.

On August 27, 2015, Blue Mountain College celebrated their convocation for the fall term. Near the end of the formal ceremony, President Barbara McMillin made a special announcement, "Next spring we will begin our first ever scholarship gala at Blue Mountain College. With the gift of an anonymous donor and the generosity of our lead sponsor, The Peoples Bank of Ripley, we have all the cost covered for our event. As a result, we have made the faithful decision to contribute all additional sponsorship revenue to the General Scholarship fund." President McMillin's comment regarding tuition assistance for the student body was met with polite applause. She continued, "While the news of the event is exciting enough; I think you will be most pleased to hear that our speaker for this inaugural event will be NFL Quarterback and ESPN analyst Tim Tebow." The students gave a thunderous response when the news of a visit from Tim Tebow echoed throughout the assembly.

It's a natural fit for The Peoples Bank to be engaged in the work of Blue Mountain College since so much of their missions overlap. What is unnatural is the level at which the bank is committed to enhancing the livelihood of the people they serve. Bobby Martin and his staff indeed have a passion for impacting others through education, faith, and economic development.

COMMON

It's November 5, 2015, and a landmark day in the life of The Peoples Bank. Mrs. Hattie Johnson is a VIP customer and is coming to renew her financial arrangements with the bank. Her portfolio is managed with pristine care by longtime Vice President, Rickey Settlemires. She walks into the private office of Mr. Settlemires at her appointed time. She accompanies her arrival with an overflowing platter of fried peach pies.

"Hey Mrs. Hattie, I could smell you coming!" Settlemires says while rising from behind his desk to embrace his VIP customer. "I've been thinking about those peach pies all day."

"They taste better than they smell, Mr. Rickey." Mrs. Hattie proclaims with a further tease to Rickey's taste buds.

"Well, I've got your paperwork all ready to setup your new loan," Rickey says while getting down to business. This has become an annual event for her and her banker. They move briskly through all the signing and are finished within a few minutes. She made the final payment on a loan which required monthly payments in an amount just under $50. While closing the books on this note, she received a new one year loan for $500.

"Mr. Rickey, you know I wouldn't be able to send my family Christmas gifts if it wasn't for this loan," Mrs. Hattie says while becoming emotional with her gratitude. "My kids in Michigan always say I shouldn't send them gifts, but I want them to know my love."

"Well I'm glad I can help, Mrs. Hattie, they are blessed to have you as their momma."

Mrs. Hattie's children had moved to Michigan when they reached adulthood forty years prior. It was there that they found employment opportunities that were not available in North Mississippi. But Mrs. Hattie stayed behind, unwilling to start a new life in a strange place. Instead she spent her working career cleaning houses for a few citizens of Tippah County. Although she and her clients share a different race, they embrace one another like family. But Mrs. Hattie is a proud person, and would never let her employers know the depth of her financial challenges. Instead, she trusts her banker to help fill in the gap when the monthly expenses outweigh the income.

Rickey is nearing fifty years of employment with The Peoples Bank. As he approaches the end of his career, it seems the little things have taken on a greater meaning. "Nowadays, I probably get more satisfaction out of a $500 personal loan, than a $500,000 business transaction." Rickey understands it is certainly important to the bank, and their local economy, to help businesses with the large loans. But the emotional reward is found in the personal loans. "That small loan is just as important to a widow who can't make it from one month to the next, as are the needs of a company." Rickey thinks for a moment and then adds, "Really it's more important. It is a matter of whether she has food on the table and her lights are left on."

When you ask Rickey Settlemires to explain the success of the bank, he doesn't ignore the banking statistics. "You know we process about 80% of all banking transactions in our area. The big banks have moved into most small towns, but for the most part they have stayed away from Ripley. I think that speaks to our impact upon the market."

Rickey also never loses sight of what real success is to him and the other officers of the bank. He makes a reference to the little man, but then rejects the term as soon as it comes out of his mouth. He quickly corrects by saying, "I think what makes us special is that we have sought to serve the common man." Rickey says this, satisfied with the description of his customers and the bank's mission.

Back at the bank, Mrs. Hattie is preparing to leave Rickey's office. She stands and begins her slow gait toward the door. Just then, her smile transforms into a contemplative expression. "You know, my kids say that they can't find a bank in Michigan that will give them a loan less than $2,000."

"I'll be, Mrs. Hattie, I'm sorry to hear that," Rickey says while displaying a quizzical reaction.

"I don't understand it, but I shore am glad y'all is my bank."

Rickey understood quite well why Mrs. Hattie's family could not receive comparable loans to her annual $500 contract. The banking industry has learned they lose money on loans less than $2,000. Rickey saves Mrs. Hattie from the details of this explanation as he escorts her out of the bank.

Offering small loans is one more way that The Peoples Bank is committed to serving their customers. Because of this commitment to the common man and woman, Mrs. Hattie is able to give her family an uncommon Christmas each year.

INVESTMENTS

As the bulletin editor for the Ripley Rotary, Kyle Smith prepares the printed programs for the weekly meeting. On Tuesday, December 1, 2015, he inserted the following title for the day's program: "The Peoples Bank's Legacy of Charitable Giving." The presenter on this particular day was Smith himself. The speaker did not swagger to the podium with a motivation to boast about his company's giving. He had been asked by a fellow Rotarian to share a few of the details behind the bank's strategy.

Smith begins his remarks with this opening statement, "The Peoples Bank of Ripley has had a long legacy of charitable giving that began with Oscar Shannon's leadership of the bank in 1961. Bobby Martin became Chief Executive Officer of the Bank in 1979; his leadership has certainly continued, and greatly increased, this legacy of charitable giving."

Smith continues with details of a precise giving strategy that has an annual budget for community distribution. In addition to sticking to their budget, the bank also has a plan for designating which causes the funds will be directed to. Smith reveals three major areas in which the bank strives to impact their community: Education, Economic Development, and Health & Wellness. Smith does not disclose the budgetary amount for contributions to the community, but good sources maintain that the total giving exceeds $200,000 annually.

Surprisingly, Smith points out The Peoples Bank does not consider community contributions as charity but rather investments. He explains it this way, "The bank looks at charitable giving as really just making investments in our community. The bank is in business to make a profit for our shareholders, and although you have to look 'outside the box,' we feel that these dollars that we contribute actually come back to us many times over—and we believe that this is reflected in our growth over the past fifty years and in our market share."

Smith's expression becomes jovial and he shifts with enthusiasm when he begins talking about another giving strategy. "One of the areas of charitable giving for which we are very proud is The Peoples Bank Charities Program. This is a program within our bank that is 100% managed by our employees." He also conveys clearly that this is not a top-down program of the bank, but a grass roots operation. "Our employees form a committee and make all donation decisions. They get out and raise the money themselves and administer the program. They elect a Chairperson each year and take this effort very seriously."

Smith informed the Rotarians that The Peoples Bank Charities gave a total of $20,642.00 to 27 different Tippah and Benton County causes in 2014. Originally founded in 2003, The Peoples Bank Charities Program has raised a total of $220,070.00. Their major fund raising event is the annual 50's Day program where employees sell hamburgers, hot dogs, cotton candy, cold drinks, and other items in a 1950's atmosphere. The employees' efforts are complimented by the bank since the company underwrites all costs for the 50's Day event. Employees are also given the opportunity to contribute to The Peoples Bank Charities out of their payroll checks each pay period. Most of the bank's employees do, in fact, dispense personal funds to the Charities program, which is a testament of how a culture of charitable giving exists at The Peoples Bank.

Smith concludes his comments with these words, "The Peoples Bank hopes to continue a legacy of giving back to the community for years to come. We feel that we directly benefit by the money we invest in our community and we hope to continue a culture of giving within our organization."

After Smith finished his presentation, a local business leader stood and shared how thankful she was that The Peoples Bank took the lead role in establishing the local community theatre. She explained that through their efforts, young people were given a place to exercise their creative nature and expand team building skills. She says earnestly, "Many young people come to the theatre as shy individuals that have never spoken before a crowd. They gain comfort and people skills that will eventually serve them professionally for the betterment of our community." She proclaimed that after just a few minutes of making an appeal to Bobby Martin, he had heard enough to be convinced of the program's merits. She completes this thought by speaking directly to Kyle Smith at the lectern, "Kyle, I know that you remember Bobby calling you into his office right after I met with him. He told you to write me a check for the funds needed to start the theatre. So please accept my gratitude, on behalf of the bank, for making a difference in the lives of so many young people and our community."

As soon as she was seated, the Superintendent of Education for the local school district stood to gain the floor. He gave thanks for how the bank has been the chief supporter for every school in his district. "Before I was the Superintendent, I once coached basketball at the smallest school in the district. Even then, the bank was always there to support, in a significant way, any needs we had."

Next, a representative from Blue Mountain College stood and expressed gratitude on behalf of the school for the bank's gracious support to their ministry of education. "The Peoples Bank is the Lead Sponsor for our annual Scholarship Gala. Because of their exceptional generosity, we are able to contribute 100% of all additional sponsorship funds to our General Scholarship Fund."

Finally, the head of the county's economic development commission shared the bank's impact for creating jobs in the community. "Many are unaware that Bobby Martin was instrumental in establishing the Tippah County Development Foundation. His leadership and the bank's support has created countless jobs for the hardworking people of Tippah County."

Health & Wellness, Education, and Economic Development. These are the areas in which The Peoples Bank concentrates their community giving. How fitting it was that representatives from each of these sectors stood to deliver impromptu and unscripted gratitude. Kyle Smith began his remarks for the day by stating that the bank stays in business because loyal customers invest in their company. It could be said that Tippah County also thrives because the bank is equally committed to invest itself into the community that it serves.

REACH

In 1972, Anna and George McLean of Tupelo established the CREATE Foundation. It's Mississippi's oldest community foundation. Eventually, the McLeans would turn over ownership of their Tupelo based newspaper, making CREATE the sole stockholder of the Journal Publishing Company.

Today, CREATE unites community leaders from the seventeen counties of Northeast Mississippi. Together, they help serve the entire region through philanthropic endeavors. Longtime board member Aubrey Patterson says this about the foundation, "Service on the CREATE board is a wonderful opportunity to support our efforts to build community throughout the Northeast Mississippi region."

Patterson served as Chairman of Mississippi's largest community based bank, BancorpSouth, from 1991 until his retirement in 2014. When announcing his retirement as CEO, the bank's board shared the following statement, "Under Patterson's leadership, BancorpSouth grew from a Tupelo-based bank with about $100 million in assets to an eight-state, 300-location financial holding company with $13 billion in assets."

Patterson has served as chairman for both the *American Bankers Association*, and the *Mississippi Economic Council*. In these leadership roles, Patterson gained a unique understanding of how economic development is profoundly impacted by community banks.

As Chair of the *American Bankers Association*, Patterson toured communities and banks all over the nation. His travels in this official capacity taught him the following lesson, "Anytime I visited an economically strong community, there was always a successful community bank." Patterson paused, and continued in a measured tone, "Or vice versa, where there was a strong community bank—the result was a strong community. The two go hand in hand."

While pointing out the importance of community banks, Patterson says the following about The Peoples Bank of Ripley, "Out of all the banks with which I've ever been acquainted, none have had a more profound impact upon their community than The Peoples Bank of Ripley."

Patterson observes further, "If Bobby and The Peoples Bank only focused on Ripley, then their legacy would be complete." He continues, "But they have expanded their efforts to impact our entire region of Northeast Mississippi."

Like Patterson, Bobby Martin, has provided exceptional leadership to the CREATE foundation. Board President, Mike Clayborne, emphasizes that Martin has impacted the region far beyond his significant financial contributions. Clayborne said, "Bobby has not only invested his resources, but he has invested *himself* into Northeast Mississippi."

The same year CREATE came into existence, a gentleman named Mickey Holliman co-founded a 42 employee furniture company at a rented warehouse in Tupelo. By 1996, he had risen through the furniture industry ranks to become CEO of Furniture Brands International. At the time, Furniture Brands was the nation's largest residential furniture manufacturer with annual sales around $2.5 billion.

On April 11, 2017, the Regional Rehab Center in Tupelo, Mississippi, honored Bobby Martin with their annual Red Raspberry Humanitarian of the Year Award. He became the first person living outside the Tupelo metropolitan area to win the award. Bobby was chosen because of his unwavering support for the entire region of Northeast Mississippi.

On the festive evening, Mickey Holliman was quoted for saying this about Martin. "If I had a problem, he would be the first person to reach out to me," Holliman speaks of Martin with the emotion usually reserved for an intimate family member. "The first thing that inspires me about Bobby is his faith in God." Holliman says to indicate Martin's secret to success begins with his reach *UP*.

Holliman continues, "Just as important as his relationship to God is how he turns his faith toward others. He applies it and uses it for good." Holliman says his friend is not afraid to reach *OUT*.

But his reach doesn't stop on the surface. Holliman points out, "He doesn't just get to know his friends, but he becomes actively involved in the lives of their family members." This is Bobby's reach *DOWN* deep into the lives of his friends.

This reflection by Holliman gives a glimpse into the secret of Bobby Martin's impact. What is his secret? Reach. His reach up to God; His reach out to his community; and his reach down into the personal lives of his employees, customers, and friends.

LEGACY

When The Peoples Bank celebrated its 90 year anniversary, on April 25, 2015, Bobby Martin said, "I want to thank all of our employees, directors, stockholders, friends, and customers for what you've done to make this company what it has been for the past ninety years. Without you we would be nothing, and we realize that."

At the closing of the celebration, the officers buried a time capsule near the bank's entrance. The objects inside will help future generations to remember the rich history of the bank. In addition, this monumental act is a symbolic commitment to the bank's future.

Like his grandfather, Bob Glover has a deep appreciation for the history of The Peoples Bank's effect upon its community, "It started with Mr. Oscar Shannon and continued with Bepaw." Glover explains, "Mr. Shannon understood that a healthy community makes a healthy bank and vice versa. We still believe the same to be true today and will continue that commitment as a community minded bank."

As of 2019, Bob Glover has been employed with The Peoples

Bank for fourteen years. He serves as the banks Investment and Security Officer and also sits on the institution's Board of Directors. Bob is well respected by colleagues for his intellect and investment prowess.

In describing what he has learned from his grandfather, Bob Glover gushes as if there are too many things to name in a one hour interview. However, he does focus on a couple of main attributes that will help cement the legacy of Bobby Martin, "Hard work and people! He excels in those two commitments." Bob learned well from his grandfather and vows to never forget how important people are to the bank's success. "We are committed to helping support our customers because if they're not successful—we'll not be successful."

Bob sees a bright future in store for the bank with his mom's leadership. Mary Childs became the President and CEO of the bank in 2012 and the bank has continued to thrive under her watch. Glover describes her as "steady" and an objective manager. "She knows how to work well with others and does not overreact when faced with a problem." Mary interacts in a more reserved manner than her father, but she holds the same appreciation for others. Glover explains, "She understands the importance of people and respects the customer and our employees for the value they contribute to our company."

In 2018, Mary Childs served as President of the Mississippi Bankers Association. At the same time, Bob Glover was President of the Mississippi Young Bankers section of the association. Bobby Martin says with a laugh, "Sounds like a setup to me." But maybe this is a celebration by bankers statewide of Martin's legacy. It is also a sign that Mary and her son Bob are committed to walking the path Bobby has placed before them.

Not trying to fill his shoes but certainly committed to continue the journey he began.

Bobby Martin has a dear friend named Vance Witt. Vance is the longtime chairman at nearby BNA Bank in New Albany. Along with their wives, they have traveled together for years to the Mississippi Bankers Association convention. According to Vance, he and Bobby are more like brothers than friends. As a past President of the Mississippi Bankers Association, Bobby Martin's impact is felt throughout the state. Vance said, "When he's no longer in banking, there'll be a big hole to fill in our state."

Bobby Martin is nearing sixty years of service to the Peoples Bank and his community. Along the way, he has poured an abundant amount of joy into others. His extra efforts will indeed have a timeless effect upon our world.

The officers and shareholders of the Peoples Bank believe the company's mode of operation has stood the test of time. They are confident that their model of banking can thrive well into the future. If you ask them, to a person, what is the legacy of the bank, you may get varying responses by the individual bank leaders. However, there is one central theme which binds all their principles together: a commitment to community leadership. They are indeed The Peoples Bank.

ACKNOWLEDGEMENTS

My wife Monya, along with our sons Noah and Luke, have been extremely supportive of me throughout the journey with this book. I am blessed to share my life with them and will always be grateful for their contribution to my joy.

My parents, Gerald and Sherry Hill, have provided wisdom and insight to this process as they have to every part of my life. I could not have asked for more loving and nurturing parents.

Charlie and Martha Spearman welcomed me into their family twenty-five years ago. Thank you for sharing your daughter with me.

Bobby Martin is a mentor, friend, inspiration, and true gift to my life. He was the primary source of this book and gave me unlimited access and support to tell the story of his life and the history of The Peoples Bank.

Reeca Elliott was tireless in her efforts as the editor of this book. She has a passion for reading and is a skilled writer. She is one of the most giving people that I have ever known, and I will never be able to repay her for the vast wealth of her contributions to this book.

I am grateful for the entire Peoples Bank family. Together, they serve their community with an unwavering commitment to improve the lives of their neighbors. Each team member I interviewed for this book was eager to assist with telling this story.

Finally, but most of all I am most grateful to God. I pray that this book will inspire people to live in the love of Christ and glorify His name.

ABOUT THE AUTHOR

Jody Hill is the President of Memphis Theological Seminary, Memphis, Tennessee. He holds a Doctor of Ministry degree in Strategic Leadership. Dr. Hill is the New York Times Best Selling author of 38: The Chucky Mullins Effect. Hill is a graduate of the University of Mississippi (B.S.), Memphis Theological Seminary (M.Div.) and New Orleans Baptist Theological Seminary (D.Min.). He and his wife, Monya, have two sons, Noah and Luke.